THE EAST AFRICAN FORCE
1915-1919

GENERAL VON LETTOW FORBACH TALKING TO GENERAL SHEPPARD ON ARRIVAL AT DAR-ES-SALAAM AFTER SURRENDER. GOVERNOR VON SCHNEE ON THE RIGHT.
GENERAL VON LETTOW (WEARING HELMET) AND MAJOR KRAUT, HIS CHIEF OF STAFF.

THE EAST AFRICAN FORCE 1915–1919

An unofficial record of its creation and fighting career; together with some account of the civil and military administrative conditions in East Africa before and during that period

BRIGADIER-GENERAL C. P. FENDALL,
C.B., C.M.G., D.S.O.

The Naval & Military Press Ltd

published in association with

FIREPOWER
The Royal Artillery Museum
Woolwich

Published by
The Naval & Military Press Ltd
Unit 10 Ridgewood Industrial Park,
Uckfield, East Sussex,
TN22 5QE England
Tel: +44 (0) 1825 749494
Fax: +44 (0) 1825 765701
www.naval-military-press.com

in association with

FIREPOWER
The Royal Artillery Museum, Woolwich
www.firepower.org.uk

The Naval & Military Press

MILITARY HISTORY AT YOUR FINGERTIPS

... a unique and expanding series of reference works

Working in collaboration with the foremost regiments and institutions, as well as acknowledged experts in their field, N&MP have assembled a formidable array of titles including technologically advanced CD-ROMs and facsimile reprints of impossible-to-find rarities.

In reprinting in facsimile from the original, any imperfections are inevitably reproduced and the quality may fall short of modern type and cartographic standards.

Printed and bound by Antony Rowe Ltd, Eastbourne

PREFACE

THE record of the doings of the East African Force here set out is not taken from official documents, I must, therefore, crave indulgence for errors. The only written record I have referred to is a kind of diary, written up at irregular intervals during the time I spent on military duty in East Africa, and giving my idea of the happenings there. By far the greater part of this is written entirely from memory. It gives the impressions that I received at the time, as one who was, to a certain extent, behind the scenes. I saw no actual fighting so have not tried to describe it. The opinions expressed, and the comments made, are entirely my own, and derived from what I saw and heard. Much of what I heard came to me unofficially.

C. P. F.

CONTENTS

CHAPTER I

EARLY DAYS

PAGE

East Africa as it was and is—Colonial Office government—Settlers and settlement in British East Africa—Essentials for success—The settler and the official—Expectation of actual fighting in Africa—Local forces—Administration—Help from India—Force C, African and Indian troops—Force B and the attack on Tanga—Task of the troops during 1915—Defence of the railway—Preparation for the coming offensive 15

CHAPTER II

FORMATION

Formation of the East African force—Sir Horace Smith-Dorrien, Commander-in-Chief—The staff—Heads of administrative services—An irregular campaign—Special service officers—Work in London—Commander-in-Chief's appreciation of coming campaign—Doubts about the expedition starting—The staff visit to South Africa —Voyage out 36

CHAPTER III

ARRIVAL

Arrival in British East Africa—The new force absorbs the old—Changes involved—Substitution of English administration for Indian—Tendencies of Indian administration—Appointment of General Smuts to succeed General Smith-Dorrien—Feeling as to his appointment—The Indian generals—The East African force as General Smuts found it—Salaita—General Smuts' plan—Action at Taveta—Advance to Kondoa Irangi—Situation there —Difficulties of transport—Von Lettow—Advance to central railway—Occupation of Dar-es-Salaam . . 53

CONTENTS

CHAPTER IV
FROM THE CENTRAL RAILWAY TO SOUTH OF THE RUFIGI

Advance from the railway—State of troops—State of railway—End of South African brigades—Advance on Tabora—Release of civilian prisoners—Their treatment—Second division at Iringa—Break-down of their transport—Advance across Rufigi—Departure of General Smuts—Appreciation—The feeling in South Africa with regard to the campaign, and its effect 74

CHAPTER V
PREPARATIONS FOR NEW CAMPAIGN

Unpleasant position for new Commander-in-Chief—State of the force—Efforts to get transport—Importance of maintaining hold on country occupied—Bases and lines of supply during rainy season—The Wintgens raid—Programme for new campaign—The supply of porters—Appointment of General Van Deventer to chief command of force—Suggested reasons for change . 87

CHAPTER VI
FROM THE RUFIGI TO THE ROVUMA

Arrival of General Van Deventer—Plans for campaign—Probable object of enemy—Reasons for above opinion—The native African soldier—The moves from Kilwa and Lindi—The fight at Mahiwa—Retirement of the enemy, over the Rovuma, into Portuguese territory—Surrender of Mahenge and part of enemy—The Portuguese attitude—The airship—Suggested reason for Von Lettow's hard fighting 102

CHAPTER VII
THE CAMPAIGN IN PORTUGUESE EAST AFRICA

Orders to carry on campaign—Only African troops to remain—Commander-in-Chief's forecast of possible course of campaign—Plans—Tactics—Reason for retention of senior officer as Commander-in-Chief—Portuguese troops—Port Amelia—Minor Portuguese officials—The

CONTENTS

natives of Portuguese East Africa—Advance inland from Port Amelia—Mozambique—Quelimane—Return of enemy northwards—Recrossing of Rovuma—Preparations to meet new situation—The Armistice—Von Lettow and Schnee in Dar-es-Salaam—The end of the East African force—Departure of General Van Deventer—An appreciation 112

CHAPTER VIII

ADMINISTRATION

Difficulties—Changing conditions: as to troops, area, labour, etc.—Shipping—Opening up new ports—Work the ships had to do—Dar-es-Salaam as main base and clearing-house—Petrol and petrol ships—Difficulties and danger of transport of petrol—Forecast of operations, even for short periods ahead, added to difficulties—Purchase of food in Portuguese East Africa—Composition of administrative staff—General Smuts, Commander of forces in field rather than in control of whole force, including administration—Personality of officers chiefly concerned with administration, and how it affected the force—Regulations and their reading—Conditions of East Africa not those contemplated by compiler of regulations—Task of I.G.C. very onerous—General success of supply 132

CHAPTER IX

MEDICAL ADMINISTRATION

Some of the problems—Early days—Developments—The base hospitals in South Africa—Effect of establishment of convalescent camps in British East Africa—Large percentage of sick—The carrier problem, and its solution—Hospitals in Dar-es-Salaam and elsewhere—Native African bibis, their use in hospitals—The Uganda native hospital corps—Mosquito brigades, and their work—Hospital ships—General remarks . . . 150

CHAPTER X

SUPPLY AND TRANSPORT

Getting supplies—Difficulties owing to transhipment in South Africa—Slaughter cattle—Fresh vegetables—

CONTENTS

                                                                           PAGE

Fresh milk—Distribution of supplies—Shortage of transport—Reason for shortage—Reconditioning of motor transport—Personnel, mechanics and drivers—Keeping balance of rations—Ordnance department—Variety and extent of demands—Some reasons for unexpectedly large demands—Mosquito nets—The Y.M.C.A., and the field-force canteens 165

CHAPTER XI

THE POLITICAL AND OTHER DEPARTMENTS

Duties, etc.—The Masai—Civil government of conquered territory—Veterinary department—Tropical diseases of animals—Field still open for discovery of preventives and remedies—Fly disease—Horse sickness—Inland water transport—Motor repair shops—The Chinese—Grave registration unit—Distances—Wild animals . 175

CHAPTER XII

CLIMATE, BUSH, AND BLACK COTTON SOIL

Effect of climate on non-tropical peoples—Variation of climate in East Africa—Malaria—Mosquito nets, and their use—Necessity of periodical change out of the tropics—The advantages bush gives the defence—How Von Lettow made use of it—The effect of bush fighting on the nerves, and some reasons for it—The general prevalence of black cotton soil on all lines—The effect on transport 186

CHAPTER XIII

NATIVE MILITARY SERVICE

Africans serving with the force—Capacities in which employed—The King's African Rifles—Scouts—Machine-gun carriers and stretcher bearers—Carriers and labourers—Human transport—The beginnings of the labour department—Development—Rations of carriers . 197

CONTENTS

CHAPTER XIV

DRAMATIS PERSONÆ AND SOME HAPPENINGS

PAGE

Well-known men—" Characters "—Big men—The I.G.C.—Posts—Kenny—Ships' captains—Pretorious—Drought—Johnny Walker—The doctor the South African men swear by—Matron, South African base hospital . . 210

CHAPTER XV

THE CAMPAIGN AND THE COLONY

The campaign—Was it a success?—Von Lettow's luck—Loss of life—The men at the front—Work behind the lines—Dar-es-Salaam—The harbour—Missions—German women—The German colony still undiscovered—What of its future? 222

INDEX 235

LIST OF ILLUSTRATIONS

	PAGE
GENERAL VON LETTOU FORBACH AND HIS CHIEF OF STAFF . . . . . *Frontispiece*	
SCHUTZTRUPPE ON PARADE . . . *Facing*	31
GENERALS SMUTS, EWART AND COLLYER . . „	57
GENERAL VAN DEVENTER, ADMIRAL CHARLTON, AND STAFFS . . . . . . „	57
THE 25TH ROYAL FUSILIERS ON PARADE AT TANGA . „	61
SALAITA HILL . . . . . . „	65
" GRIDIRON " CUT IN ROAD AT SALAITA . . „	65
DAR-ES-SALAAM AND HARBOUR . . . . „	73
BRITISH G.H.Q., DAR-ES-SALAAM . . . . „	73
" STUCK " ON THE ROAD TO THE RUFIGI RIVER DURING THE RAINS . . . . . „	83
INDIAN TROOPS CROSSING LUMI RIVER . . „	83
MOTOR TRANSPORT ON BLACK COTTON SOIL . . „	97
LABOUR CORPS, AN AMMUNITION COLUMN . . „	97
THE KAISER'S BIRTHDAY, DAR-ES-SALAAM . . „	109
A GERMAN ASKARI REGIMENT ON THE MARCH . . „	109
A GERMAN MACHINE-GUN IN THE BUSH . . . „	125
MILITARY HOSPITAL, DAR-ES-SALAAM . . . „	159
KAISERHOF HOTEL ANNEXE AS HOSPITAL, DAR-ES-SALAAM . . . . . . „	159
MOTOR TRANSPORT CAMP, DAR-ES-SALAAM . . „	159
KING'S AFRICAN RIFLES AT DRILL . . . „	201
A K.A.R. SIGNAL SECTION . . . . . „	201

MAP

SKETCH MAP OF THE EAST AFRICAN CAMPAIGN AREA . „ 15

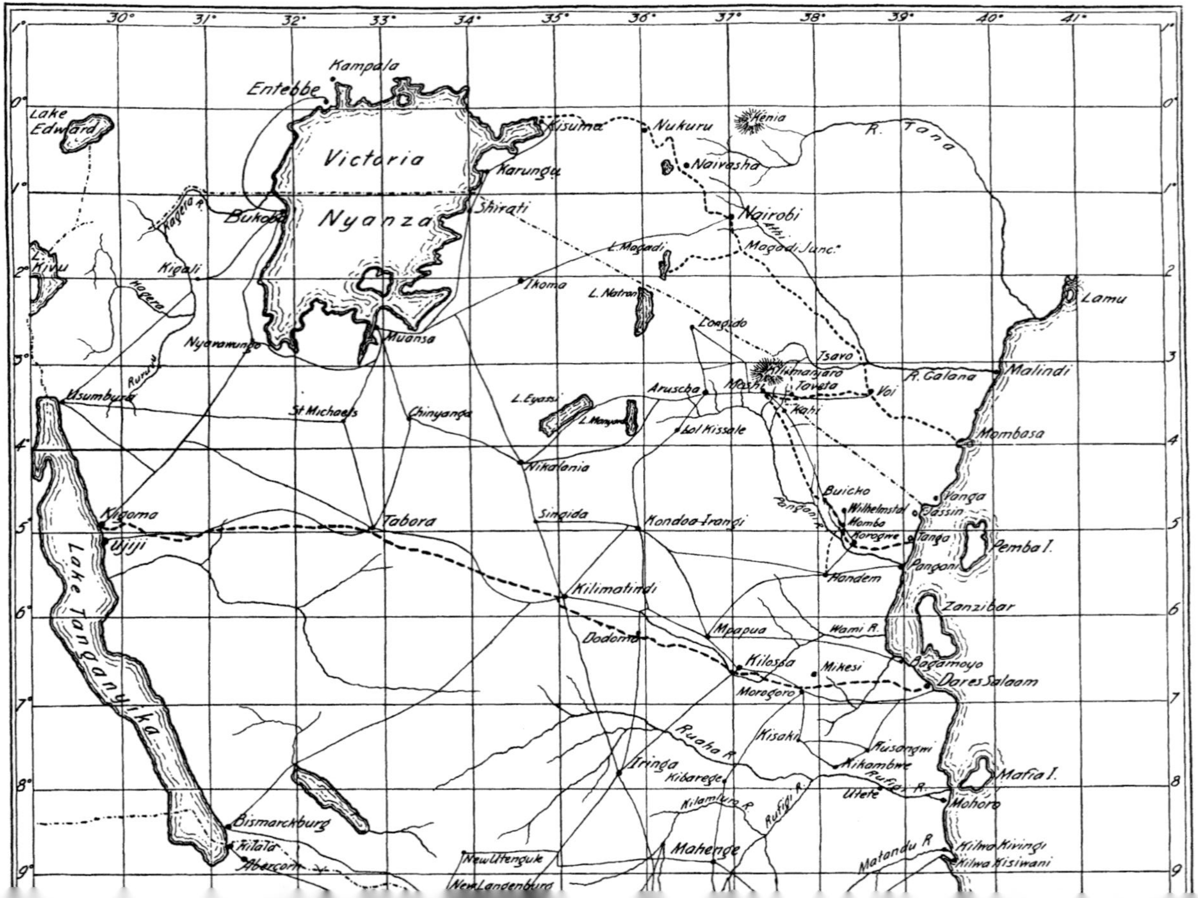
30°
31°
32°
33°
34°
35°
36°
37°
38°
39°
40°
41°
1°
0°
2°
3°
4°
5°
6°
7°
8°
9°
Kampala
Entebbe
Lake Edward
Victoria
Nyanza
Kisumu
Nukuru
Kenia
R. Tana
Naivasha
Karungu
Shirati
Nairobi
Athi
Magadi Junc.
Kagera R.
Bukoba
L. Magadi
L. Kivu
Kigali
Kagera
Ikoma
L. Natron
Lamu
Longido
Muansa
Nyaramungo
Rurugu
Tsavo
Kilimanjaro
R. Galana
Malindi
Usumbura
Aruscha
Moshi
Taveta
Voi
L. Eyasi
Kahi
St Michaels
Chinyanga
L. Manyara
Lol Kissale
Mombasa
Nikalania
Buicho
Pangani R.
Wilhelmstal
Vanga
Mombo
Jassin
Kigoma
Tabora
Singida
Kondoa-Irangi
Korogwe
Tanga
Pemba I.
Ujiji
Lake Tanganyika
Pangani
Handem
Kilimatindi
Zanzibar
Mpapua
Wami R.
Dodoma
Kilossa
Mikesi
Bagamoyo
Dares Salaam
Morogoro
Ruaha R.
Kisaki
Rusongmi
Iringa
Kikambwe
Mafia I.
Kibarege
Rufiji R.
Utete
Mohoro
Kilamluro R.
Rufiji R.
Bismarckburg
Mahenge
Kilwa Kivingi
Kilala
Matandu R.
New Utengule
Kilwa Kisiwani
Abercorn
New Landenburg

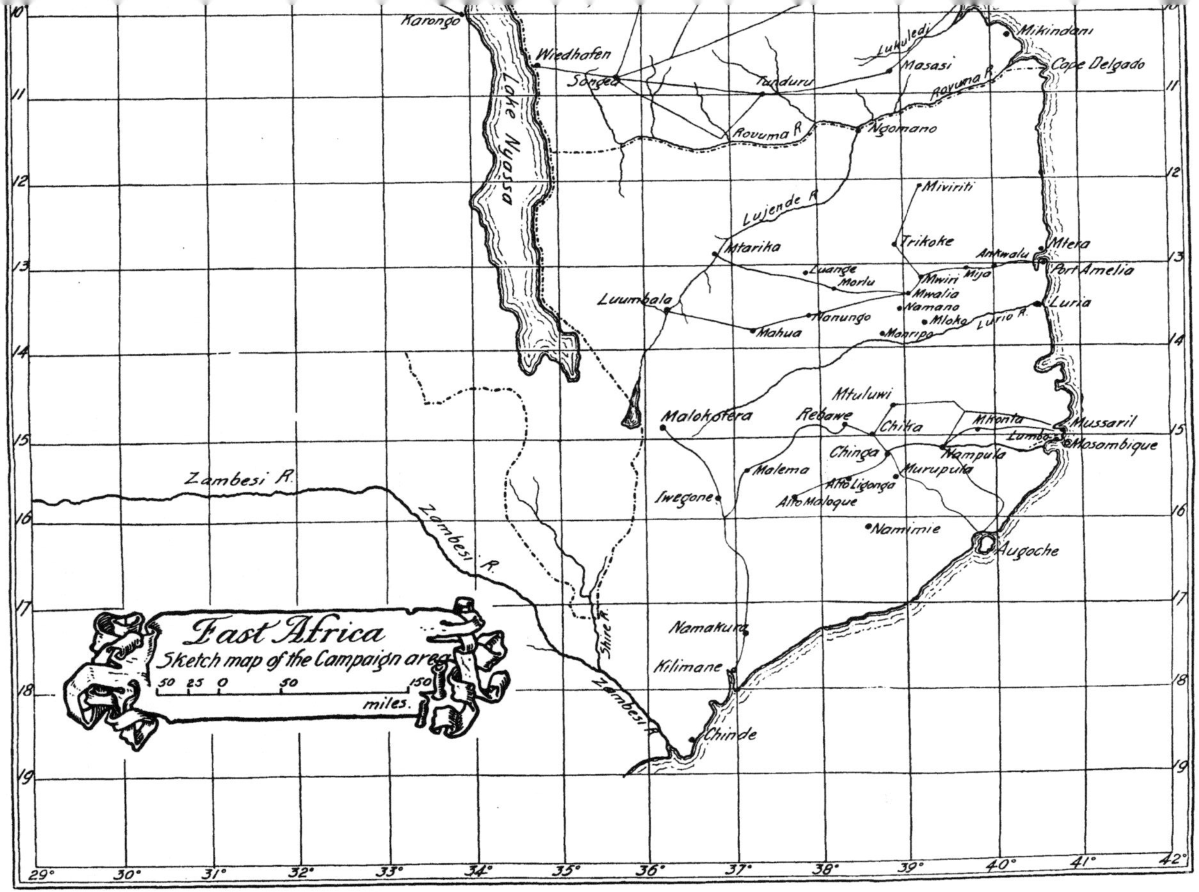

East Africa
Sketch map of the Campaign area
50 25 0 50 150
miles.
Lake Nyassa
Karongo
Wiedhafen
Songea
Tunduru
Lukuledi
Masasi
Mikindani
Cape Delgado
Rovuma R.
Ngomano
Miviriti
Lujende R.
Mtarika
Trikoke
Mtera
Ankwalu
Port Amelia
Luange
Morlu
Mwiri
Mija
Mwalia
Namano
Luumbala
Nanungo
Mloko
Luria
Lurio R.
Mahua
Monripo
Mtuluwi
Malokotera
Rebawe
Chitka
Mkonta
Mussaril
Lumbo
Mosambique
Chinga
Nampula
Malema
Murupula
Alto Ligonga
Alto Moloque
Iwegone
Namimie
Augoche
Zambesi R.
Shire R.
Namakura
Kilimane
Chinde
29° 30° 31° 32° 33° 34° 35° 36° 37° 38° 39° 40° 41° 42°
10 11 12 13 14 15 16 17 18 19

THE EAST AFRICAN FORCE
1915-1919

CHAPTER I

EARLY DAYS

East Africa as it was and is—Colonial Office government—Settlers and settlement in British East Africa—Essentials for success—The settler and the official—Expectation of actual fighting in Africa—Local forces—Administration—Help from India—Force C, African and Indian troops—Force B and the attack on Tanga—Task of the troops during 1915—Defence of the railway—Preparation for the coming offensive.

To the great majority of stay-at-home Englishmen East Africa is in the nature of an unknown country. At one time, during the war, they probably did notice that it was talked of in the papers, but all interest was soon lost in matters nearer home, and which affected them more closely. Some there were who came in contact with men who had been soldiering out there, and who said that it was a poisonous country. That was the end of their knowledge. Possibly they might remember having heard, when it was recalled to their minds, that East Africa was the country of the " Man-eaters of Tsavo "; or, if they were interested in religious discussions, that there had been a good deal of ecclesiastical trouble over what was called the Kikuyu conference, and that Kikuyu is a district of British East Africa; or, if of a sporting turn of mind, they would know that it is a part of the world to which rich men were in the habit of going on big game shooting expeditions. As for any idea of what sort of country it is, how big it is, or where exactly it lies on the continent of Africa, they have none. Actually the British Empire has very valuable and very extensive interests in East and Central Africa. British East Africa and Uganda have, together, an area of about four hundred thousand square miles—rather more than three times the area of the British Isles—with a population of about six and a half millions. These countries are only beginning to be developed, and there can be no doubt that they both have great futures before them.

As regards their position on the map, the Equator runs through both countries. British East Africa is mostly south of that line and Uganda north of it. Generally speaking British East Africa extends from the sea to Lake Victoria, and Uganda to the north, north-west and west of that great lake. They together border on the Sudan to the north, what was German East Africa to the south, and the Belgian Congo on the west. The northern boundary of British East Africa is generally the Juba River, where it borders on Italian Somaliland; the southern boundary is an artificial one agreed on with Germany

EARLY DAYS

about twenty-five years ago. The nature of the country changes as you get away from the coast. Along the coast there is a low-lying, hot, damp but fertile strip, where cocoanut palms grow well. Then comes a dry strip of almost waterless bush country, with the elevation above the sea constantly increasing. The country here becomes fertile again, with open plains covered with grass, and country fit for coffee and sisal. Four hundred miles from the coast the land rises to some seven thousand feet above the sea—on the edge of the great rift—then drops almost precipitately some three thousand feet, continues so for a hundred miles, rises again to eight thousand feet, and drops again gradually in the next hundred miles to the level of Lake Victoria, about four thousand feet above the sea-level. Uganda lies more or less at the level of the lake. It is a fertile country, with much soil suitable for growing cotton. In British East Africa there is much land suitable for coffee, sisal, wheat, flax, and possibly sugar-cane; there are also vast stretches of valuable forest land, and open grass land suitable for stock farming.

Thirty years ago there was only one way of getting from the coast to Lake Victoria, a distance of nearly six hundred miles. One had then to march on foot or on horseback, a journey that took three months to perform, and which was none too easy, the dry stretch being bad to cross. Now a railway runs from Mombasa, the port on the coast, to Kisumu, the port on Lake Victoria, in under forty-eight hours. Thence well appointed steamers cross the lake to the

Uganda ports. The railway was a great engineering triumph. The crossing of the Great Rift Valley, with its almost precipitous, three thousand feet sides, was a puzzle that took a lot of solving.

Both territories, British East Africa (now called the Kenia Colony) and Uganda, are under the Colonial Office, and the Colonial Office government has methods of its own. Firstly, it, till recently, grossly underpaid its officers whilst placing them in positions of great responsibility; secondly, the last thing it seems to desire is the development of the countries under its charge. The Uganda railway was built when these territories were administered by the Foreign Office. Uganda made a special appeal for exceptional treatment by any British Government. It stands as the great example, the great triumph, of missionary enterprise, for its inhabitants are mostly Christians. The two great rivals in the mission field, the Church Missionary Society and the Roman Catholic Church, share the country between them. Even the Royal Family is divided in religion; the reigning king is a Protestant, his cousin and heir presumptive a Catholic. At Kampala, the capital of the Kingdom of Uganda, several of the hills on which the town is built are crowned with the headquarter-buildings of the missions. How could any British Cabinet turn a deaf ear to the appeal of such a country for some means of access to the sea. All the Colonial Office seems to ask of a local government is that it shall pay its way. For a Governor to look ahead, to wish to undertake works which must result in increased prosperity to the country he governs within a very few years, unless he can pay for them out of current revenue, seems to be a crime. The man who earns the goodwill of the permanent officials, and so is sure of promotion, is he who jogs along patiently, obeys orders, asks for nothing, and does nothing. The enterprising man soon finds that his transfers are not to more pleasant, or more lucrative, appointments. It is only since the war that a loan of a substantial amount has been made to Kenia Colony for the development of the harbour at Mombasa, one of the most backward ports in the British Empire; and for the construction of a branch railway that will bring many hundreds of square miles of fertile land, fit for settlement by Europeans, within reasonable distance of a market. Both these works ought to have been undertaken at least ten years ago.

A good many of the settlers in British East Africa were originally attracted to the country by the big game shooting. They then saw possibilities; they had capital; land was obtainable on very easy terms; they took up grants, some to grow coffee, others sisal; others turned their attention to raising stock. The French missionaries had shown the possibility of growing coffee of as fine a quality as any grown in the world. In fact, the coffee of East Africa mostly originated from seed supplied by the French Fathers near Nairobi.

By degrees a considerable area of the country was settled by white men. Not all were of the class that came originally to shoot big game. Many were retired officers of the Navy or Army. Among others were Boers from South Africa, settlers in a small way who were given land on the Uasin Guishu plateau beyond the Rift Valley. Some of the settlers took up very large areas, and spent much money on developing their properties and experimenting in different industries.

In all industries there are two essentials to success: plentiful labour at a reasonable cost, and access to a market. The settlers claimed, with some justice, that they were the real force that was developing the country, and that upon them depended the value of the country as a part of the Empire. They considered that government ought to do a great deal more than they were doing to assist them, especially with regard to the two essentials mentioned. As regards the first, the government held that the native of the country was entitled to first consideration, and that he must not be compelled to work for the benefit of the white settler. The African native in his natural state has few wants. With the aid of his family he can cultivate sufficient land to supply the household with food. Clothes are not an expensive item with many tribes; skins of animals make an efficient covering for those who consider any covering at all necessary. If the native has any other wants the necessary money can be earned by a very few days' work. The advent of Indian traders, who set up shops all over the country and displayed goods which pleased the natives, helped to set up a desire to buy. To buy it was necessary to have money; to get money it was necessary to work. Labour became fairly plentiful. Settlers who treated their labour well could get, and keep, labour. The great majority of the settlers were men who were naturally inclined to treat their labour well, but there was a minority who did not do so. The government, therefore, made rules concerning native labour which were intended to protect the native in such cases that required protection, but the settlers declared that these rules were so framed that they could be read as giving power to district officials to interfere with the free flow of labour to the well managed estates, and by so doing take away the authority a master should have over his men. They also complained that some district officials did not hold the scales of justice even in disputes which came before them between masters and men, but unduly favoured the native, so treating all settlers as if they belonged to the undesirable class. This led to much ill feeling between settlers and officials. In pursuance of the former's ill will against the latter, the settlers, led by some of their number—men of position and influence —exceeded all bounds. No official could do right, and every act of an official was subjected to criticism of a very unfair character. Everything was done to make the lot of the official unbearable. That there were faults on both sides is allowed. The settlers had real grievances in the neglect of the Colonial Office to open up the country, and in the way the labour ordinances were interpreted and administered by some of the officials. The local officials had every right to complain of the way the campaign was being carried on. Under the circumstances it was not to be expected that the officials would strain the law in favour of the settlers.

During the years just prior to the war there were great accessions of all kinds to the ranks of the settlers. Settlers properly so-called, farmers, i.e. producers; shopkeepers, i.e. importers; export agents and dealers in local produce, i.e. distributors; and, what is said to be a sign of growing prosperity, lawyers. Nairobi became a considerable town, with good shops, hotels, etc. There were other good-sized white settlements at places like Naivasha and Nakuru, in the Rift Valley. All over the high, and comparatively healthy, uplands farms were being established.

There was an idea that, should war break out between England and Germany, there would be no actual fighting in Africa, and there was good reason for thinking this. Everyone connected with administration or colonisation of savage Africa believed that the tradition of the inviolability of the white man must be maintained if a few hundred whites were to continue to impose their authority, in governing many thousands of blacks, in safety. It was thought that it would be most dangerous to employ black troops to fight against white men; even to the extent of employing black troops trained and officered by white men against black troops similarly organised. It was feared that the prestige of the white man

EARLY DAYS

would be lowered, and that the progress of civilisation in Africa would be put back a hundred years. The prevalence of this idea led to the maintenance, both in British and German East Africa, of only sufficient troops to deal with local risings, and, in the case of British East Africa, to protect the tribes on the northern frontier from the incursions of the turbulent Somalis over that border. For the Somalis considered their more peaceful brethren of our territory fair game, as did wandering bands of Abyssinians from farther afield.

Each Protectorate in East and Central Africa had a small military force of its own, not police, composed of native African soldiers, and officered by men seconded from regular British regiments, for a limited term of service under the Colonial Office. These Protectorate battalions were known collectively as the King's African Rifles. For some years, up to 1913, there had been four battalions; the first and second raised in Nyasaland. Of these the second was employed on the northern frontier of the British East African Protectorate. The third battalion belonged to British East Africa, and the fourth to Uganda. These battalions were very efficient units; the officers were mostly adventurous spirits of a sporting turn of mind, who had got tired of regimental soldiering in peace-time, and had turned to service in less civilised parts of the world than those they had been accustomed to. They were the very best stamp of British regimental officer. These battalions were organised as such, but, beyond that, there was no military organisation, and they were administered by the civil governments to which they belonged. All departmental affairs were in the hands of the civil government. There was, thus, no military nucleus on which to build the administrative services required when serious military operations had to be undertaken.

About the end of 1913 the Colonial Office had ordered the disbandment of the second battalion, and at the outbreak of war this had been nearly completed. All that remained was a remnant, still on the northern frontier, of men who were to be transferred to the first battalion, and absorbed into it. When war came the whole military force in the East and Central Africa Protectorates amounted to three battalions of King's African Rifles. There were, however, considerable numbers of police; men of the same class as the askaris of the King's African Rifles, and trained as soldiers up to a point, though not organised as a military force.

The idea, so widely held, that no military operations would be undertaken in Africa was at once dispelled. The safety of the country against possible enemy raids had to be assured; the danger of such was real. The frontier line between the protectorates, British and German, runs roughly parallel with the Uganda railway, and not very far from it. Along the railway were the chief European settlements. Considerable anxiety was felt for the safety of these settlements. It was thought that it was on them that the enemy would be likely to make

EARLY DAYS

attacks, and the forces available for their protection were anything but adequate. Alarming rumours were set afloat that enemy aeroplanes had been heard over Nairobi; that enemy parties were on the move, and that promises of rewards had been made to the askaris should they make a successful attack on the white settlements.

Immediately war was declared the Governor issued an appeal to all Europeans to give their services in defence of the Protectorate. Before the appeal reached the outlying settlers many had left their farms, and were on their way to Nairobi to offer their services in any capacity. Many of these settlers had invested their all in their farms, and were working hard to make their undertakings paying concerns. It was only constant personal supervision that could achieve this end, but all had to be left to unreliable overseers. To all it meant serious loss, to some it meant absolute ruin. The women did their share; in many cases the wives of settlers pluckily remained on the farms, surrounded only by natives, the nearest white man or woman being many miles away, and carried on. One lady settler took over the superintendence of five or six farms belonging to neighbours who had gone off to serve, and carried on her self-imposed task for a long time with marked success. She rode almost incredible distances every week to see that all was going well. Later on arrangements were made for settlers who were unfit for active service to look after groups of farms whose owners were away, but it was not altogether a success. Many settlers, though they escaped absolute ruin, found the labour of years thrown away and had to start all over again.

Two settler corps were raised at once, a regiment of mounted rifles and one of infantry. As many of the settlers had been in the army there was no lack of men to undertake the training of these corps. In addition to these two, more or less, regular units scout corps were raised to watch the long frontier; from Boers settled on the Uasin Guishu, from Somalis settled in the Protectorate, and from some of the wilder tribes. These corps were commanded by men who knew the country well, and the men under them. Arrangements were made for the Masai to watch that part of the frontier which passed through their country, and to bring reports to their officers whom they knew and trusted. On the coast Wavell, a very remarkable man of an adventurous disposition (he was said to have been to Mecca as a pilgrim) raised a corps of Arab Rifles, at the head of which he met his death in action some eighteen months later. He was a man the Arabs of the coast almost worshipped. The police force was drawn on to form a battalion for service on the northern frontier, and in order to set free the King's African Rifles serving in that inhospitable region. In the main centres of white population defence corps were raised, and every able-bodied white man, who, for any reason, had not been able to join the active corps, was called on to join and be trained for defence. High officials and settlers in all ranks of life served side by side in the ranks.

By virtue of his letters of appointment the Governor was Commander-in-Chief; he was therefore responsible for all measures taken to raise local forces, and for all operations. He and the Governor of Uganda acted together, and the senior officer of the two battalions in the combined territories was placed in command of the troops under him. As the troops were all either Colonial Office units or troops raised under the orders of the Protectorate governors the fact of a civilian being Commander-in-Chief did not much matter at this time. The Governor was believed not to have much liking for soldiers, but he was wise enough to appreciate that the situation was one with which it was imperative professional soldiers should deal. He, therefore, established martial law, and acquiesced in the majority of the proposals put before him by his chief military adviser, the officer commanding the troops, though he was unable to conceal his dislike of all it meant in the dislocation of his civil government. It may be maligning him, but the general feeling on the spot seems to have been that he unwillingly accepted the necessity for such dislocation rather than willingly place all the resources of his government at the disposal of the man who, under him, was responsible for the defence of a British population against what looked like a serious danger.

Administration had to be improvised; civil departments had to assume military duties where analogous civil departments existed. The civil medical department and the civil transport department were already accustomed to see to the wants of the King's African Rifles when medical assistance was wanted, or the troops had to move about the country. The heads of these departments were given military commissions by the Governor, and their departments were organised to meet the new situation. Supply departments did not exist; equipment, clothing and all ordnance stores were sent out by the Crown Agents for the Colonies on yearly indents direct to battalions. The King's African Rifles askari fed himself in peace time, and was fed regimentally when on active service. There was no need in peace for ordnance and commissariat, and there were no analogous civil departments. The necessity, at the time, was to get what was required and to get it quickly. Nor was it likely that anyone would know where the things required were to be got better than the men engaged in the trade concerned. It thus came about that accepted principles had to be scrapped, and men bought for government things in which they themselves dealt, in fact bought from their own firms. It speaks well for East African business men that there were very few complaints either of the quality of the goods supplied, under these circumstances, or of the price paid.

The Protectorate was not left long without help, for, after a short time, a small force arrived from India to assist in the defence. The officer

EARLY DAYS

commanding this force was a General, and thus became the senior officer of the force in East Africa, though, of course, under the Governor, who still remained Commander-in-Chief. The situation now became quite different. The first Officer Commanding troops belonged to the Colonial service for the time being, the new one was an officer of the Indian army commanding an Indian expeditionary force; the latter's position was, therefore, somewhat anomalous. The two forces under his command were serving under different conditions, for there were two administrations working alongside one another, in the same area, on totally different lines. The situation was not made easier by the want of understanding between the two forces. But it is easy to understand why there should be misunderstanding if the Indian situation in East Africa is realised. There were a good many Indians in the Protectorate; the Uganda railway had been built with Indian labour, and was worked by the same; many of these workmen had settled down in the country and were working as artisans. Indian traders in a small way had spread all over the country; there were small Indian shops everywhere; there were also contractors and big shopkeepers from India in all the larger towns. The only Indians East Africa knew were men of the trading and artisan class, and they were not liked, and consequently looked down upon. The small tradesman was there to make money, the artisan monopolised the profitable work. Both settlers and natives thought that the Indian soldier was the same sort of man as those they knew, whom they hated and despised. The Indian soldiers knew nothing of the African. They did not believe that they could be compared with the native of India as a soldier. They looked upon the Protectorate force as a force of irregulars, which the members of the force very naturally resented. Under these circumstances it was not astonishing that the relations between the two forces were strained.

The first small force was followed a few months later by quite an important one. The first force had only been sent to strengthen the defence, the second had a much more ambitious rôle assigned to it, namely, to gain a footing in German East Africa by the capture of Tanga. This town is a port on the coast, just south of the frontier line, from which the Usambara railway starts to connect Moschi, the summer headquarters of the German administration on the slopes of Kilimanjaro, with the sea. Much of the country between Tanga and Moschi was occupied by German settlers who were cultivating coffee, sisal, and rubber on a considerable scale.

The attack on Tanga was a miserable failure. Delays occurred which did away with the element of surprise on which the success of the enterprise, as planned, largely depended. The enemy were able to get troops down from the Moschi area to defend the town, which they did successfully, defeating the attack with heavy loss. There was nothing to be

GERMAN SCHUTZTRÜPPE ON PARADE, GERMAN E. AFRICA.
(From a captured photograph.)

EARLY DAYS

done but re-embark the troops and depart to British East Africa. Whether the failure was due to bad staff work, failure on the part of the troops, want of whole-hearted co-operation on the part of the Navy, or a combination of all three, need not be discussed here. Considering the numbers of troops available for the attack it is not surprising that the failure to take the place was regarded by the Protectorate force as confirmation of the estimate they had formed of Indian troops. This estimate was still further confirmed by what took place in an action at Longido, on the west of Kilimanjaro at about the same time. A mixed force of Protectorate and Indian troops came in contact with a German force there, and the behaviour of some of the Indian troops did not favourably impress the Protectorate men.

After another action at Jassin, on the border near the coast, at the end of the year, which was also a failure, though very nearly a success, as had been the attack on Tanga in spite of unfortunate happenings, the force had to resign itself to a defensive rôle for many months. A successful attack was made on Bukoba, on the west shore of Lake Victoria, and there were many minor actions along the frontier, some successful, some the reverse.

For the greater part of the year 1915 the situation changed very little, the two forces faced one another, neither being sufficiently strong to risk an invasion in force. The Uganda railway, the only line of communication between the interior of the country and the coast, was very vulnerable, and that it should be preserved from serious damage was of vital importance; its defence was, therefore, one of the chief tasks of the force. For many miles the track runs through thick bush country, almost uninhabited. The bush grows close up to the line and stretches for many miles on each side, on the south right down to the German frontier. The enemy mode of attack was to send raiding parties from their posts along the frontier to lay mines in the permanent way. The activity of these raiding parties was curtailed by the absence of water in the bush, for they had to carry sufficient to last them to the railway and back. The mines they laid were arranged to explode when a train passed over them, and to minimise the damage empty vans were run in front of the engines, so that if an explosion did occur the damage was done to a comparatively unimportant van and not to a vitally important engine. To prevent these raiding parties reaching the line at all was impossible, the most that could be done was to hold all important points, such as bridges, with fixed garrisons, and patrol the line constantly with parties of armed men, with the twofold object of intercepting the raiders and discovering and rendering harmless any mines they had laid. There were a good many encounters with raiding parties either on the line, or in the bush when they were being followed up on their way back, or intercepted on their way to the line. Following up was very difficult; it was very hard to find tracks in the dry bush. Bloodhounds were tried, but the

EARLY DAYS

dryness of the bush was too much for them also.

As a general rule the raiding parties came from the enemy posts on the frontier, did their work and went straight back, but one party discovered a water hole to the north of the line and settled down there for some days. Our troops knew there was a party about, but naturally hunted for them to the south of the line. It was a bold and resourceful move on the part of the Hun. He caused a good many derailments with his mines, in spite of careful patrolling, but no really serious damage was done, and the defence of the railway was a success. The loyalty of some of the Indians in British East Africa came under suspicion at this time. The railway was using wood as fuel for their engines. This was cut and collected by Indian contractors, who, with the natives employed in cutting the wood, lived in huts along the railway. These men were suspected of harbouring the enemy raiding parties, and some were tried and severely punished. There was extra reason for doubting the loyalty of some of the Indians in the country as a great deal of correspondence with the seditious party in India was going on. But it is a little difficult to see what an unarmed Indian is to do when a German with a party of armed men comes to his hut and demands water and shelter.

In the latter part of the year the energy of the force was directed towards preparing for an advance into German territory, and as soon as sufficient troops could be made available. There are not many lines by which any considerable force can pass from British to German East Africa or vice versâ. Along the coast an advance is possible, when, for about eighty miles, the dry bush country intervenes. Beyond this there are the two routes, one on either side of Kilimanjaro. The route that had most attractions for the General in command of the force was that to the east of the great mountain. It led straight to Moschi and the head of the Usambara railway. By it Tanga could be reached down the valley of the Pangani River, or an advance made over practicable country to the Central railway, and the main settlements of the German colony. The enemy knew that it was only a matter of time before an advance would be made, and that we were only waiting until sufficient troops could be collected to ensure success. The starting of a railway from Voi, a station on the Uganda railway about a hundred miles from Mombasa, showed him by what route the advance would be made. To oppose such advance the enemy took up a position on the north-eastern spurs of Kilimanjaro, at Taveta, an area actually on the British side of the frontier. In addition to the railway the road from Nairobi to Longido was put in order that a force might be placed there to advance south-eastward round the mountain, and cut in behind the Taveta position, the idea being that the two advances would be made together; the main force from rail-head on Taveta, the subsidiary force from Longido. The Longido route was not a very favourable line for the advance of a large

EARLY DAYS

force as there were doubts about the supply of water.

By the end of November the G.O.C. was able to report that the arrangements for the concentration of the force, as soon as the fresh troops arrived, were complete; the railway was well advanced; camps were ready, and transport had been collected. There was already a considerable force at rail-head facing the enemy in the Taveta position, with an outpost on a detached hill at Salaita. Early in December the enemy succeeded in surprising the detachment at Salaita, drove them out, and occupied the hill themselves. There they remained until the general advance took place three months later.

CHAPTER II

FORMATION

Formation of the East African force—Sir Horace Smith-Dorrien, Commander-in-Chief—The staff—Heads of administrative services—An irregular campaign—Special service officers—Work in London—Commander-in-Chief's appreciation of coming campaign—Doubts about the expedition starting—The staff visit to South Africa—Voyage out.

By the middle of 1915 the oversea possessions of Germany, with the one exception of German East Africa, had been taken from her, and it was obviously undesirable that this, by far her most important possession in Africa, should be left in her hands. In East Africa itself things seemed to be at a deadlock; the one serious attempt to get a footing in the country, the attack on Tanga, had been a failure. A considerable number of British troops were in British East Africa, but the force was not strong enough to conquer the German colony. England was full of troops training, but they were all wanted for France. India had her hands full; her troops were in France, in the Dardanelles, Egypt, and in Mesopotamia; beside those already sent to East Africa she could not find enough good troops to make up the latter force to a strength that would ensure success. The Union of South Africa was in different case. The rebellion which had broken out in that country, shortly after the beginning of the war, had been crushed by the energetic action of Generals Botha and Smuts; so completely crushed that the rebel element in the population was not inclined to cause active trouble again for the present. The same two great men had conquered German South West Africa. South Africa was, therefore, in a position to offer help to the Empire in any way desired. Advantage was taken of this readiness to help by a suggestion to send troops for the conquest of German East Africa. The idea was taken up with some enthusiasm in the Union. Steps were at once taken to raise and despatch a force of a brigade each of mounted troops, field artillery and infantry, with ambulances, hospitals and auxiliary services.

It is now known—it was more or less an open secret at the time—that it was the intention of the home government that the chief command of the force to be employed in the conquest of German East Africa should be given to a South African General, but that neither Botha nor Smuts was then able to accept the appointment. Though the political situation was quiet enough for them to be able to send troops it was not stable enough for either of the great political leaders to take their hands off the wheel of the ship-of-state for the length of time it was possible the campaign might last. It was recognised from the first that the campaign would be a difficult one to bring to a satisfactory conclusion; that, and the fact that the force would include a contingent from the Union, made it imperative that the officer appointed to the command must be a man of great ability and prestige. General Sir Horace Smith-Dorrien was in England at the time, without anything to do; he was offered the appointment and accepted it. No more happy appointment could have been made. General Smith-Dorrien has a wonderful personality; he was just the man to inspire the troops in East Africa with the spirit that would make them a victorious fighting force. It must be remembered that for many months these troops had been acting on the defensive, following on a disastrous repulse, that their encounters with the enemy in minor operations during this time had not been invariably successful. In addition, they had been serving in a tropical climate for a long time, and had suffered much from fever and other tropical diseases. There was every reason, therefore, to suppose that they might not be a first-class fighting force, either morally or physically. There is nothing like coming under a leader whom everybody knows to be one of the best, in whom everyone has unbounded confidence, to make a force that has had discouraging experiences pull itself together, and show what it can do when properly led. As a matter of actual fact, though the state of morale varied considerably it turned out to be very much higher than it had been thought likely to be. The feelings of South Africa generally, and of the

FORMATION

men of the contingent especially, deserved consideration. The news of the appointment was received in that country with acclamation. It was gratifying to their pride to know that the officer under whom the Union contingent was going to serve was a man of Smith-Dorrien's prestige, a man considered by all soldiers one of the finest Generals in the British Army. South Africans of all races admired him. In the infantry of the contingent there were many Englishmen who had served during the Boer War; some actually under his command. All knew the splendid reputation he had for his work there. The Boers in the mounted brigade had an equally great respect for him, and admiration for him as a soldier; though, of course, their experience of him was gained from the other side, for many of the men had served against us.

The East African Force came into existence in November, 1915. The force was to include all the troops in East and Central Africa, all the troops being sent from South Africa, and it was hoped at the time that it would include some units serving in England. The staff was ordered to assemble in London, and the G.H.Q. unit, clerks, batmen, motor drivers, etc., was ordered to be mobilised at the Tower. Captain Guest placed some rooms in his house in Park Lane at the disposal of the Commander-in-Chief, for use as an office, and until it was time to sail.

Included in the staff were men of very varied experience. The Chief of the General Staff was

Simpson Baikie, a gunner, a staff college man, who had been on General Smith-Dorrien's staff on Salisbury Plain. He was now just home from Gallipoli, where he had been commanding the artillery of the 29th Division. Another gunner who had been on Simpson Baikie's staff in Gallipoli, also a staff college man, was appointed G.S.O.1. He went straight out to East Africa without coming to London. The G.S.O.2 was a man who had served with the King's African Rifles, and brought to the staff first-hand knowledge of the country, its soldiers and conditions. Captain Guest was appointed G.S.O.3. As head of the administrative side Brigadier-General Ewart, an officer of the Indian Supply and Transport Corps, who had been serving with the Indian contingent in France, and had previously served on Army Headquarters in India, was appointed D.A. and Q.M.G. The A.A.G. was a gunner, on the retired list, of long regimental experience, who had been serving on the staff in England since the beginning of the war. The A.Q.M.G. was an officer of the Indian Army who was already holding the appointment in East Africa; he had served on the staff in India before the war.

All the men appointed as heads of the administrative departments had some special qualification for their appointments. Hazelton, who was appointed Director of Supply and Transport, had special knowledge of motor transport, besides having had experience in administration. As motor transport was expected to play a very important part in the campaign his special knowledge was bound to be useful. Hunter, the Director of Medical Services, had come from India with the Indian Cavalry Corps. His experience of medical administration was probably unique for a man of his service (he was still a Colonel), for he had twice held the position of Director of Medical Services in the Egyptian Army. Scott, head of the Ordnance, had been serving at the War Office, and so knew, and was well known to, all the heads of his service. Not a bad asset for a man who would have to make many extraordinary demands. The Director of Remounts had only lately given up a similar appointment in South Africa, and so was thoroughly conversant with the horse markets of that country from which the force was to draw all its animals. The Provost-Marshal had served in the early stages of the war with the King's African Rifles. Crowe, a staff college man, was C.R.A., and Dealy, a military works man, who had come from India with the Indian contingent, was C.R.E.

Officers already serving in East Africa were appointed to command the divisions and brigades into which the force was to be organised. They were mostly holding similar appointments. The officer commanding all troops in British East Africa was appointed to command the 1st Division. The important position of Inspector-General of Communications was given to Captain (temporary Lieutenant-Colonel) Edwards, the Inspector-General of Police in British East Africa and Uganda. His special qualification for the post was his knowledge of the country and the natives.

It was perhaps rather astonishing that a staff, with so much of what might be called irregular experience likely to be of use, could be got together for a side show at such a time, and so quickly. The work the staff had to do was to conduct a campaign of an " irregular " nature; irregular in the sense that it would be carried on in a country for the most part uncivilised; irregular in the sense that the troops were to a large extent not regular soldiers. Looking into the antecedents of that staff it will be found that it contained men who had seen service wherever the British Army had been employed during the past thirty years; Burma and the Indian frontier, Egypt and the Soudan, South, East, and West Africa, France and Gallipoli.

Apart from active service there were men who had been on the staff in most parts of the world. To direct the operations of, and administer successfully, this very mixed force the staff had to deal with, knowledge of English staff methods, Indian administration, and local African conditions of warfare, were all wanted. The men with special knowledge of each, in several cases with special knowledge in more than one of the lines mentioned, were there. One man could supplement the knowledge of another. The various elements of the staff seemed to fit together like the bits of a jig-saw puzzle, where each bit is a necessary part of the

FORMATION

picture, and fits into its place to complete the picture; its irregularities of outline fitting into similar irregularities in its neighbours. In fact, more than like the regular shaped bits which go to make up a parquet floor, where every piece is complete in itself.

Taking the " irregularity " of the campaign into account, and the many odd jobs there would be to do, the Commander-in-Chief considered that he would want as many men who had a knowledge of the country, its language and its people, as he could find. The special work for which it was thought men would be wanted was intelligence work, for which it did not seem likely there would be any too many men with the necessary qualifications—ability to speak the language and get on with the natives. It was also thought at the time that irregular corps of natives would be wanted, and officers with similar qualifications would be wanted for them. There was also likely to be a call for officers to take charge of the districts of German East Africa as they were occupied. There were a good many men serving in England and France at that time who had served at some time in East Africa. Some in the King's African Rifles before the war, some during the early stages, either in the King's African Rifles or in the irregular Protectorate corps raised under the governor's orders. The Commander-in-Chief proposed to take out as special service officers a considerable number of these men if they were willing to come, could be spared, and were suitable.

It soon became known in London that there was a chance of getting out to a show that promised to be more interesting than the trenches in France and Flanders during the winter, and that the call was for men with a taste for adventure. In consequence a lot of men came to Park Lane to offer their services. Some had claims to consideration—they had been out in the country—others had none. Some certainly had the one claim that they were adventurous spirits. For instance, one man based his claim on the fact that he had been chief of the staff to General Villa in Mexico. The Commander-in-Chief did not think that, from what he had heard of Villa's methods, that his chief of staff was suitable. Another claimed that he was the only Englishman who knew one particular bit of German East Africa. This looked promising, but it turned out that he had gained his knowledge as an elephant poacher; that his antecedents were at least doubtful, and that warrants were out against him for poaching, and other offences against the law, in every Protectorate in East and Central Africa, and in some of those in West Africa as well. It was not considered advisable that he should go.

The War Office was not sympathetic about special service officers, and it was only after much discussion that an establishment of eight was sanctioned. This meant that a good many who would have been very useful, and were very anxious to come, had to be left out. The eight chosen were all men likely to be useful in the sort of jobs for which they were wanted. Six of the eight were men who had had previous experience in the country, either as settlers, or as big game hunters. There was one very notable man who knew as much about East Africa, the country, the people, and the game, as any man living. Cunninghame, the best known white hunter in the Protectorate. A quiet mannered, blue eyed man, he was noted for his extraordinary courage, and his coolness in emergencies. He had done marvellous things in the course of his career as a hunter of wild animals. Not only did he know British East Africa from end to end, but he knew many parts of German East as well. He was one of those men, few and far between they are, who can get to the back of the black man's mind. Another was Verbi, a missionary and a Bulgarian. He had been in charge of a mission station near Taveta, a place in the hills near the camp where the main force was to collect. He had an immense influence over the wild men amongst whom he had lived and worked. During the early part of the campaign he had done very good service, getting labour from the country round his mission, and as an intelligence officer. The War Office rather demurred to giving him a commission as he was an alien enemy by nationality, but agreed in the end as there were so many men able to speak to his loyalty, and the value of the services he had rendered. Two of the others were ex-officers of British cavalry; one, a settler in British East Africa in earlier and less civilised times, would certainly have won fame as a buccaneer and soldier of fortune. He had travelled all over East Africa, from Abyssinia down to German territory, trading and shooting. The other was a restless spirit, craving excitement and change, doing his jobs well but soon tiring of them. He had just returned from service with the Cossacks in the Carpathians, had served in several other theatres of war, and, after a time, left East Africa to serve in yet more theatres, becoming, for a change, a regular soldier. He earned distinction in that capacity. The other two who knew the country were settlers to a modified extent. They both had interests in the country, and had lived out there, but were not men who made it their home. One was interested in a gold mine in Madagascar, the other had been serving with the Royal Naval Division in Gallipoli. There was a young officer of the Rifle Brigade who made good later in a very difficult position. And last, but not least well known, there was Major Josiah Wedgwood. Always ambitious, he had left politics temporarily—though he said he had in that sphere just reached a position he really liked, that of leader of a party of which he was the only member—to show what armoured cars could do in a bush country.

The three weeks the staff spent in London were three weeks of very hard work. It was astonishing what a lot of things there were to see to and arrange with the War Office and the Admiralty. The Commander-in-Chief explained what he hoped to do on arrival in East Africa. The official information from the G.O.C. on the spot was fairly clear and informative, with the addition of that which the many men in London, who had lately returned from there, were able to give him. The Commander-in-Chief was thus able to arrive at a fairly accurate appreciation of how matters actually stood. He made a special point of his confidence that, when all the reinforcements which had been promised arrived on the scene, he did not anticipate very great difficulty in defeating the enemy in the field, though he could not help having doubts as to the quality of some of the troops to be sent.

The newly raised South Africans were, to a certain extent, an unknown quantity. Some, by no means all, of them had fought in German South West, and, even if they had, this campaign was going to be a very different experience, covered as so much of the country is with dense bush. They were, therefore, likely to be raw and inexperienced for the most part. The white troops which had been some time in the country were known to be suffering badly from fever and other tropical diseases, to say nothing of the lowering effect of the tropical sun. The Indian troops were in like case. The African troops were few in number. The G.O.C. in East Africa was rather pessimistic about the state of health of the troops, and the effect it had had on their morale.

The Commander-in-Chief expressed his opinion that the real difficulties to be afraid of were the country and the climate. By the time he was due to arrive in the country the rains would be very nearly due, when the country would become impossible for active operations for several months, and the climate in the low-lying parts so poisonous to Europeans that, to keep them there, would simply mean rendering them unfit for anything in the nature of active service for an indefinite time. His idea was that, on arrival, he would attack the enemy at once and drive him out of British territory, gain the high ground round the great mountain, Kilimanjaro—the Moschi area—and make himself secure there. He realised that, in order to make himself secure, it might be necessary to occupy positions in the low unhealthy country, but he hoped that, by a system of frequent reliefs, he would be able to save the men from being badly knocked up by the climate. The time of enforced abstention from active operations would then be used for making preparations for a further advance as soon as the country was dry enough. He said it was impossible to judge as to what would be done later, until he had seen the situation himself, and on the spot. He told the heads of departments that what they were to prepare for was the advance to the Moschi area, and the maintenance of the force there, and in the neighbourhood, during the rains. By the time the rains forced a halt he hoped to have his plans settled, and that he would then be given time to prepare for a further advance. He said that he was convinced no good end could be reached in using up troops by working them in the rainy season in a country like East Africa.

This appreciation, added to by information gained from official and unofficial sources in answer to telegrams sent, and questions asked of men who knew the country, gave the heads of departments something pretty definite to work on. Knowing that the heads of the various services on the spot were officers of Indian departments, and that, therefore, it was more than probable that the requirements of the force had been underestimated, or at any rate that the margin allowed was a very narrow one, the heads of services made their demands a good deal larger than the position, as officially reported, seemed to warrant. They were quite right.

Up to almost the last moment there were doubts as to whether the expedition, on the scale proposed, would really go out. There seemed to be considerable difference of opinion as to the advisability of committing the country to the conquest of German East Africa at that particular time; to the starting of an enterprise which might want a lot of feeding to make it a success. Lord Kitchener was not in favour of it, and was disinclined to guarantee the Commander-in-Chief the minimum force with which he was willing to act. There were, however, powerful interests at work in favour of the expedition starting, and, at the last moment, matters were arranged, and a start made.

At first it had been intended that all the staff, with the exception of the Commander-in-Chief and his chief of staff, who were to go viâ South Africa to consult General Botha and the South African government on various points, should go out in the *Persia* viâ Aden. But when that ship left London the question as to whether the expedition was to go or not was not definitely settled. This delay was rather lucky for the staff as the *Persia* was torpedoed in the Mediterranean on that voyage. When things came to be discussed it was found that there were so many points to be gone into with the South African authorities, as that country was to be the main source of supply for the force, that it was essential all heads of services should have a chance of going into them on the spot. Arrangements were, in consequence, made with the Union Castle line to take out the whole headquarters on the next mail steamer. This happened to be the *Saxon*, sailing from Plymouth the day before Christmas. The heads of the Union Castle line were most kind, doing everything to make matters easy, and offering the chief as much accommodation as he wanted. But the headquarters of even a small force such as his amounts to a good deal. The total number of officers embarking was forty-three; there were also between one hundred and fifty and two hundred warrant officers, non-commissioned officers and men, and in addition a lot of motors and baggage. The Admiralty made arrangements for a fleet auxiliary to meet the headquarters at Durban, and take them on to Killindini.

Headquarters left Paddington at midnight 23rd-24th December, 1915, and arrived at Plymouth in the early morning, to find a high cold wind blowing. It was possibly this cold which laid up the Commander-in-Chief. He had had a bad influenza cold for some days, but was then much better than he had been. He came off to the ship in the afternoon in a piercing wind, against which there was no shelter in the tug. That evening he seemed fairly well; next day he was ill; a day or two later he was desperately ill. When the ship reached Cape Town he was just able to crawl out of his cabin, and down the gangway, looking about as bad as a man can look and be alive. The force saw no more of him. It was not realised by all, though probably it was by the doctors, that there was no chance of his being able to come on after a short rest at the Cape.

All the heads of services disembarked at the Cape, and went up to Pretoria to settle the points they had for discussion with the Union officials, and the heads of departments of the defence force. Many decisions were come to and many arrangements made. On paper these looked excellent, but depended for their success on whole-hearted co-operation on the part of all concerned. This they did not get. The heads of services of the East African Force cannot be blamed for entering into the arrangements they did. These ought to have worked well, and they would have done so had not obstacles been put in the way of their smooth working by people over whom the East African Force had no control.

At Durban headquarters were transferred to the *Trent*, a fleet auxiliary, which put into Lorenzo Marques to pick up the heads of services travelling there from Pretoria, and then proceeded to Killindini, arriving there on January 27th, 1916.

CHAPTER III

ARRIVAL

Arrival in British East Africa—The new force absorbs the old—Changes involved—Substitution of English administration for Indian—Tendencies of Indian administration—Appointment of General Smuts to succeed General Smith-Dorrien—Feeling as to his appointment—The Indian generals—The East African force as General Smuts found it—Salaita—General Smuts' plans—Action at Taveta—Advance to Kondoa Irangi—Situation there—Difficulties of transport—Von Lettow—Advance to central railway—Occupation of Dar-es-Salaam.

THE force in East Africa was called Indian Expeditionary Force B, organised on Indian lines, commanded by a General of the Indian Army, and staffed by officers on the Indian establishment, for the most part officers of the Indian Army. There had been a good many changes in the chief command during the year after the force, and subsequent to its abortive attack on Tanga, had landed at Mombasa. At the end of 1915 the General in command was a man very well known in India, an impetuous and energetic Irishman who had seen much fighting in various parts of the world, and had the reputation of being a first-class fighting man. A soldier never so happy, never so cool and collected, as when actually under fire. His soul must have sorely chafed at being confined to a defensive rôle, and his mind at being called upon to make preparations for a campaign which would now be carried on by someone else. He had settled down to the work, spared neither himself nor others, and had got everything well advanced by the time the necessary troops arrived in the country. He must have been pleased that the plans he had made for opening the new campaign were accepted in principle, very nearly in detail, by the man to whom it fell to carry them out.

The formation of the East African Force, with a Commander-in-Chief with full powers, raised the status of the expedition. The force was changed from an Indian Expeditionary Force to an Imperial Force, carrying out operations directly under the War Office. Indian Expeditionary Force B lost its individuality and was absorbed in the new organisation. Its General in Command became a divisional General. The officers who had been heads of departments became subordinates to the directors of services appointed by the War Office. The new staff was, at least, a grade higher than the old. The Chief of the general staff was a Brigadier-General general staff instead of a general staff officer class one. The head of the administration a Deputy-Adjutant and Quartermaster-General instead of assistant. The heads of services were graded as directors instead of assistant directors. Most of the staff and departmental officers of the old force were appointed to the new with gradings as high, or higher, than those they had been holding; but, of course, in some cases, instead of being heads of their services, they came under officers of superior grading who had come from England. Some of them showed very plainly that they did not like it, and it was natural that they should not, but there was no need to show it quite as aggressively as they did. What they disliked as much as losing their places at the head of services was being brought under English ways of working in place of Indian. With the exception of these departmental officers everyone seemed pleased at the change, glad that, at last, there was a chance of something being done, and that there was a staff in the country to cope with the work.

Up till now the force had been starved; staff officers had been much overworked, and there were very few clerks. The force had increased in size gradually, and the staff had not been added to in proportion. The troops, owing to the nature of their duties, could not be properly organised in self-contained divisions and brigades, consequently a great deal of work that would ordinarily be disposed of by subordinate formations had to be done by G.H.Q. How the work was as well done as it was astonished everyone.

Indian administration has a leaning towards over-centralisation; heads of departments concern themselves with details which ought to be dealt with by subordinates, and thus leave themselves no time to attend to their proper work of superintendence. Good administration is arrived at when the head of a service lays down principles and leaves details to his subordinates, contenting himself in seeing that the work is properly done, and the principles not departed from, but, at the same time, being always ready to help a subordinate in difficulty about his work, and to give a ruling on a doubtful point. Indian administration also made a fetish of economy by putting it before efficiency, which is clearly wrong. Efficiency must be regarded as the goal to be attained, most certainly with economy; for, in the long run, efficiency means economy. To attain efficiency forethought and imagination are needed. In India heads of services were tied down to a hand-to-mouth existence; rigid scales governed everything; only the narrowest margins were allowed. Such a system can be made to work well in peace time, but in war it is liable to lead to disaster. Unfortunately it was so ingrained in the minds of Indian departmental officers that they were unable to rise above it when the occasion so demanded. They were afraid to look ahead, afraid to order anything more than would suffice to bring the meagre reserves, as laid down, up to scale. No proper allowance was made for the extra wear-and-tear of active service; no provision was made for increase in numbers which they knew was certain.

Early in February the news arrived that General Smith-Dorrien had resigned the command of the force through ill health, and that General Smuts had been appointed to succeed him. The first intimation was received in a Reuter telegram,

GENERAL SMUTS (CENTRE) WITH GENERAL EWART (LEFT) AND GENERAL COLLYER, C. OF S. (RIGHT).
ADMIRAL CHARLTON, GENERALS VAN DEVENTER, SHEPPARD AND SOME MEMBERS OF THEIR STAFFS.

which also gave the information that the command had been offered to General Smuts in the first instance, and before General Smith-Dorrien had been appointed. The same day an official telegram announced the appointment of General Hoskins, who, just before the war, had been Inspector-General of the King's African Rifles, and therefore knew the country, to succeed Simpson Baikie as Brigadier-General general staff. Everyone was disappointed at the news that General Smith-Dorrien was not able to take over, but there was no room for astonishment.

It is of no use pretending that the appointment of General Smuts was not a bit of a shock to most people. Everybody knew that he was a great force in South Africa; Botha's right hand man in peace and war, but very few knew anything more of him. The heads of services who had met him at Pretoria on the way out had been much impressed by him, and by his helpfulness and knowledge of what would be required. There was a good deal of speculation as to what he would do. Some thought he would get rid of all the staff and put in men of his own from South Africa; the reason for such an idea being that he was used to their ways of running a campaign, and not to those of a regular British Army staff. As soon as he arrived he made it plain that he had no such idea in his head. His chief anxiety was that everything should be carried on strictly according to War Office ideas, so that there could be no cause for complaint against the administration.

But the question as to the general staff became a different matter altogether. He had brought some staff officers with him, and it soon became apparent that he wished to have one of these, Colonel Collyer, as chief of his general staff. As it is generally accepted that a Commander-in-Chief is entitled, if not actually to choose his chief of the staff, to at any rate have a very decided voice in the matter, he probably did not feel in any way bound to acquiesce in the appointment made by the War Office. At first the War Office did not seem inclined to agree to the setting aside of their nominee, but eventually gave way, with the proviso that an equally important appointment should be found for General Hoskins, and suggested that General Tighe, who had been in command of the troops in East Africa for some time prior to the appointment of a Commander-in-Chief, should return to India, where his services were wanted, and that the command of the division thus vacated should be given to General Hoskins. By the time this suggestion was made General Smuts had had an opportunity of discovering the worth of the Indian Service Generals with the force, and had decided that two of them must go. One of these was quite a good man and a capable commander, but he had failed to carry out a task entrusted to him to the satisfaction of the Commander-in-Chief. Finding himself unable to carry out his orders to the letter he had taken what the Commander-in-Chief evidently considered the wrong alternative. The Commander-in-Chief felt, after this, that he was not a man whose judgment he could trust. The other was a man who never ought to have been given a command in the field. He had had very little experience in command of troops at all, and had failed on more than one occasion, once rather badly and just before General Smuts arrived. These two were being sent away because the Commander-in-Chief had no further use for them. The case of General Tighe was quite different, and the Commander-in-Chief was very anxious there should be no chance that anyone should think he was in the same boat as the others. He was well aware of the good work General Tighe had done in preparing for the advance. He had seen at Taveta how well he could handle troops in action. Strong representations were therefore made to the War Office with the result that, before he left the command, General Tighe was made a K.C.M.G.

The South African contingent received the news of General Smuts' appointment with somewhat mixed feelings. The mounted brigade, composed almost entirely of Boers—loyal Boers be it understood—and commanded by one, were, very naturally, pleased. General Smuts was one of themselves. The infantry, largely composed of Englishmen, were not so enthusiastic about it. They would have preferred General Smith-Dorrien. Politics are a very active force in South Africa; for, though the two loyal parties in the Union were working together in support of General Botha's policy, there was a good deal of racial jealousy. They did not quite relish having to serve under a man of the other race. The rebel Dutch hated Smuts, but they were very unlikely to serve as soldiers of the Empire in any force, whether commanded by an Imperial General or a loyal Dutchman.

The force which General Smuts found on his arrival in the country was quite a considerable one, though composed of many different elements. The local forces raised at the beginning of the war were still in existence, though considerably reduced in numbers. When the arrival of troops from India made the Protectorate safe from attack a good many men were allowed to go to Europe, to serve in France and elsewhere. The King's African Rifles remained at the strength of three battalions, one in British East Africa, and one in Uganda in addition to the one in Nyasaland. The original Indian Expeditionary Force had been reinforced by some first class fighting battalions which had served in France, had been badly cut up there, but had since been brought up to strength again with recruits and reservists. There was one regular British battalion which had come over with Force B, and had been at Tanga; one service battalion, the 25th Royal Fusiliers (The Frontiersmen), raised and commanded by Driscoll, who had made a name for himself as the commander of Driscoll's scouts in the South African war, and had since been connected with the Legion of Frontiersmen in London. This battalion had come out from England. A white regiment had been raised from among the settlers in Rhodesia and

THE 25TH ROYAL FUSILIERS (LEGION OF FRONTIERSMEN) ON PARADE AT TANGA, 1917.
(The late Capt. Selous marked with a cross.)

ARRIVAL

sent up. There were a squadron of Indian cavalry and two Indian mountain batteries, an Indian volunteer heavy battery and machine gun company, various Indian infantry battalions, some regular, some Imperial service, a battery manned by settlers in British East Africa, and various ambulances, hospitals, and other auxiliary services, Indian and African. All the above had been in the country some months. Just arrived was the South African contingent, a brigade each of mounted troops, field artillery and infantry, with auxiliary services of all sorts, including a base hospital which was stationed at Nairobi.

The troops were divided into two main parts. The larger was collected at Mbuyuni—the rail-head of the military railway branching from the Uganda railway at Voi—to face the main German force in position at Taveta. The smaller was at Longido, about eighty miles due south of Nairobi, north-west of Kilimanjaro, and on the opposite side of the mountain from Taveta. The mounted brigade and the South African field artillery were in camp near Nairobi completing their equipment. Line-of-communication troops were still watching the railway. In Uganda the 4th King's African Rifles, a regiment of Indian infantry, and a battalion of police were watching the Kagera River, the boundary between British and German territory west of Lake Victoria.

A few days before General Smuts arrived in the country an attack had been made on the enemy's position represented by the hill at Salaita, the post the Germans had captured on the fifth of December. It was not a success. The artillery preparation had been wrongly directed, and was therefore quite ineffective. The South African infantry, when sent to make the attack, came under machine-gun fire and failed badly. They learnt lessons, however, which were very good for them. The Indian in South Africa is disliked more even than he is in East Africa for similar reasons, with the addition of an economic reason. Owing to his lower standard of living he is, as a small trader, able to undersell the white man. The South African troops, on their arrival, were very contemptuous of the Indian soldier, spoke of him as a coolie, and expressed very freely their disgust at having to fight alongside him. When the South African infantry were held up at Salaita, and thoroughly scared, (it was their first time under fire) it was an Indian infantry regiment which came to their assistance and pulled them out. Thereafter, though they said little, they could not help regarding the Indian soldier with a different eye. This was for the best, for they had to fight alongside one another for many a long month.

The first thing General Smuts did on landing, and before coming to headquarters at Nairobi, was to visit the troops at Mbuyuni and Longido. From what he learnt on his visit to the former he came to the conclusion that the enemy position at Taveta was not as strong as it had been stated to be. It was too big for the force the Germans had available to occupy it, and the flanks were not secured by natural obstacles. The original plan, made before his arrival, was for an advance from Longido, round south eastward behind Kilimanjaro, of a combined force of infantry, in strength something more than a brigade, and the whole of the South African mounted brigade. The fact that the country between Longido and the mountain was more open, and therefore more suitable for mounted action than that near Taveta, no doubt had its influence in the making of this plan. The idea was for this force to get on the road beyond Moschi and cut off the retreat of the enemy in the direction of Aruscha when he had been driven out of the Taveta position. General Smuts decided to modify this plan to a certain extent. He did not abandon the idea of a double advance, but he decided to use the mounted brigade for a less extended flanking movement on the right of the main attack on Taveta, leaving the infantry force to carry out the wide turning movement by itself.

The plan finally decided on was to make a frontal attack on the Taveta position with the main force, whilst the mounted brigade, supported by some of the field artillery and South African infantry, made a fairly wide turning movement round the enemy's left, among the lower, northern foothills of Kilimanjaro. The force at Longido was to advance round the mountain, so timing this advance as to arrive on the Moschi-Aruscha road just in time to intercept the enemy should he try to retire that way. The amount of opposition the Longido force was likely to meet was not known, but it was judged that it would not be very serious as the Germans were not likely to be able to spare many men from the defence of the main position. Very little was known of the roads on that side of the mountain, but it was known that roads did exist. The force started in what seemed to be ample time to get to its destination by the time ordered, but got into very bad country, found the roads almost impassable, and was late at the junction of the roads.

The main attack was successful. The enemy retired from their position at Salaita when they found that the advance of the main force would cut them off from their main body. They also abandoned the Taveta position, evidently realising that it was too extensive for them, and that it was turned by the advance of the mounted brigade, so retired to a position farther back in the bush-covered hills at Latema. Here they put up a stubborn resistance. The attack was to have been commanded by General Malleson, but he was too ill to take charge of the operation, so General Tighe, who was in command of the division, took personal charge.

The first attack was held up, and various reinforcements put in; for, though each carried the line a bit forward, they failed to carry it up to the actual position before nightfall. After dark some of the Rhodesians got into the position, and when daylight came the enemy were found to be in general retreat. They did not retire due west in the direction of Moschi and Aruscha but south-west

SALITA HILL. A KEY POSITION DEFENDING ROAD INTO GERMAN EAST
AFRICA, CAPTURED MARCH, 1916.
"GRIDIRON" CUT IN ROAD AT SALITA TO PREVENT PURSUIT BY
ARMOURED CAR.

in the direction of Kahé. The mounted brigade met some opposition in their turning movement, but easily overcame it. Subsequently, they got into very bad ground in the foothills, and were unable to get up in time to interfere with the enemy in his retirement. The casualties were fairly heavy; among the killed was Colonel Graham commanding the 3rd battalion King's African Rifles, an officer of the Indian Army (The Guides) who had seen much service in Africa, and knew more about fighting in Africa, and the fighting man of that country, than anyone. He was a great loss. The South African infantry here behaved very well.

The question now was, " What next? " The enemy had been forced to retire from the little bit of British territory he had been occupying. The Moschi-Aruscha area was in our hands, for the mounted troops had gone on there at once. But, though the enemy had been forced to retire, he was by no means demoralised; his retirement had not been interfered with. The situation was very much that which General Smith-Dorrien had anticipated, and with which he had said he would be satisfied until the rains were over. There was every indication that the rains were very near. During the rains movement is almost impossible, and the climate in the plains more than unhealthy for Europeans, indeed for all troops. General Smuts came to the conclusion that, in order to consolidate his position, it was essential to occupy some position from which he could dominate the Masai steppe extending a hundred to a hundred and twenty miles south of the Moschi-Aruscha area to Kondoa Irangi and Handeni; also that the enemy must be pushed eastward down the Pangani valley beyond Kahé. To achieve the former the mounted brigade was sent to Lol Kissale, forty miles south of Aruscha, where they succeeded in rounding up an enemy detachment. The nature of the ground made it evident that there would be considerable difficulty in keeping up supplies, even for that distance.

Instead of remaining at Lol Kissale the mounted brigade pressed on to Kondoa Irangi, sixty miles farther south. They there came in contact with an enemy detachment, but did not succeed in rounding it up as they had that at Lol Kissale. The administrative staff made a strong protest against troops being placed so far away during the rains, pointing out that the roads were almost impassable already, and that when the rains were fully on they would almost certainly be quite so. The suggestion that the mounted brigade should be recalled to Lol Kissale was not entertained. It must be allowed that the move to that place was justified by the necessity to dominate the Masai steppe, but there is little doubt that the presence of a strong mounted force there would have achieved that object. Under these circumstances the forward move to Kondoa Irangi cannot be justified. It meant that a body of troops was isolated on the far side of a piece of country a hundred miles wide, over which supply was bound to be almost impossible for several months. At the time the move was made there was every reason to think that supply would be quite impossible, and it was only the discovery of another road that made it possible.

Von Lettow was a very clever, far-seeing man, as well as a trained and accomplished soldier. It is plain that at this time, and for long afterwards, his aims and intentions were not realised at G.H.Q. The general idea was that he would look on the defence of Dar-es-Salaam, Tabora and the central railway, as his main object, for which he would fight to the last, and that their loss would mean the end of the campaign. Later it became evident that such was not his idea, and never had been. He thought that he could best serve his country's interests by so acting that we should be compelled to keep as large a force as possible, for an indefinite time, in East Africa, and that the action most likely to effect this was to fight delaying actions only, and to avoid risking the destruction of his force in a general action fought to a finish. He saw very clearly that the ultimate fate of the German colony would not depend on the result of the campaign in East Africa, but on the result of the war as a whole. He knew that his chance of preventing our occupying the colony, if we had made up our minds to do so, as apparently we had, was remote. It was unlikely that any more ships, with arms, ammunition and stores for his force, would be able to slip through the blockade of the coast the Navy was trying to make effective—he had been very lucky up to now in that way—and that he would be dependent upon what he had in hand, what could be produced in the country, and on what he could capture from us and from the Portuguese; the latter especially. In addition to delaying us as much as possible by rear-guard actions he always kept his eyes open for a chance of attacking any detachment he thought he could overwhelm. In the detachment at Kondoa Irangi he now thought he saw such a chance. He knew the country, knew what it was like in the rainy season, and judged that we should have great difficulty in keeping up supplies for even a small force there. The mounted brigade there alone must have seemed to him delivered into his hands. The movement of troops to the support of this brigade would be difficult in itself, and he had good reason to think that the supply of a force of sufficient strength to defeat his object would be impossible; therefore, he judged that reinforcement was in the last degree likely.

The mounted brigade had not been at Kondoa long when it became evident that they were not going to be left in undisputed possession of the place. Forces were being collected against them, and the numbers of those forces were constantly increasing. Von Lettow probably thought he had plenty of time; he knew that a considerable period must elapse before we should be able to make a serious advance with the main force down the Usambara valley, and that he was safe in withdrawing troops from that front for the enterprise against Kondoa. He thought he could carry that through and have his troops back again in time to meet the advance when it came.

G.H.Q. became very anxious about the safety of the mounted brigade, and determined that, in spite of everything, it must be reinforced. The South African infantry brigade from Himo was ordered to Kondoa. There was very little transport available for the move—just sufficient to carry rations for the march. For the kits there was none available at the moment. As it is impossible for heavily weighted men to do long marches in a tropical climate kits had to be left behind, to be sent on as soon as transport could be found. The idea of the officers with the infantry was that the transport would be available almost at once, and that the kits would catch them up in a day or two. The men marched with just the clothes they stood up in, and a waterproof sheet apiece. They did not even take greatcoats.

The roads were in a terrible state; the rains were full on; the transport had to be helped along, and seldom arrived till quite late in the evening, often after dark. For twenty-three of the twenty-six days they were on the march it rained almost continuously round the twenty-four hours, the men, therefore, never had a chance to get dry. The rations were unsuitable for such conditions as they required cooking. To cook rations properly in the dark and rain is almost impossible; especially when wood is hard to come by—as it was in many places—and, when found, very wet.

In addition to being always wet the men were always hungry. At every post where it was possible to leave men numbers were dropped, sick, done up, and with sore feet, for their boots gave out badly. A portion of the column struggled through to Kondoa, and had to go straight into the trenches. But they were in time.

Von Lettow had made a miscalculation. The place had been reinforced before he could assemble sufficient forces against it to make a successful attack. The troubles of the unfortunate infantry were, however, by no means at an end. Though a new road had been discovered, over which a very much curtailed supply would be able to be kept up, it was not yet in working order. This meant the establishment of a new base, and the transfer of transport. For a fortnight after the arrival of the infantry no supplies reached Kondoa. The men had to live on a stock of very inferior rice left behind by the Germans, and what could be got from the country round. Luckily there was plenty of fresh meat to be had. But the establishment of the new line did not mean full rations for these unfortunate men, and it was only a very reduced ration, from which all the extras had had to be cut out, that reached them.

ARRIVAL

Hospital accommodation was very indifferent, to say the least of it. The South African doctors were not great at improvisation, and a genius in that way was wanted there to make things tolerable. If such a man had been there much might have been done. Evacuation of bad cases was impossible over that road, so had to remain where they were. With only just sufficient lift on the road to keep up a restricted supply of rations it was impossible to send up hospitals. Field ambulances had to do the work of stationary hospitals; clothing and equipment could not be sent up in anything like sufficient quantities to supply the wants of the men; most of the kits never arrived at all. A certain amount of food was available in the country round, but the arrangements made by the South African staff for getting it in, and distributing it, were bad. Enterprising men with money to pay for it got some extra food, and the mounted men did best as they were able to get farther afield. As time went on the ration improved a little, but the men never got the full field ration to which they were entitled during the two months they were there.

Von Lettow, all the time, was increasing his force before the place, and keeping up his threat of attacking it in force. G.H.Q. began to get nervous again, and, in order to create a diversion, hurried on the advance down the Usambara valley, turning it southwards in the direction of Handeni, before everything was ready.

Previous to his arrival in East Africa General Smuts had arranged for the recruitment, and sending up of a second mounted and a second infantry brigade from South Africa. These new brigades arrived in time to take part in the advance of the main body. Large reinforcements had come up for the original contingent, and were sent forward to Kondoa, together with horses to remount the mounted brigade. The Boer is not a careful horsemaster, and the horses of the mounted brigades died at an appalling rate. The first mounted brigade had been remounted at least twice before the advance from Kondoa.

When the new South African contingent had arrived, and the country had had time to dry up a little after the rains, a general advance was ordered. The general direction was due south; the force at Kondoa being directed on Kilimatinde and Dodoma; the main force on Morogoro; all places on the central railway. The Kondoa force found themselves opposed by what they took to be the rear-guard of the force which had been in front of them for such a long time, but, in reality, the main body of that force had been withdrawn to join the enemy main body, which was opposing the advance of our main force. The Kondoa force reached the central railway and turned eastwards along it, whilst the main force advanced more slowly towards Morogoro, as they were meeting with considerable opposition from the enemy.

But Von Lettow avoided anything like a

DAR-ES-SALAAM AND HARBOUR.
BRITISH G.H.Q., DAR-ES-SALAAM.

decisive action, skilfully withdrawing time after time as soon as he saw that there was sufficient force on the spot to drive him away if he did not go of his own accord. He should have been brought to a standstill, and forced to fight it out, on more than one occasion, had the second mounted brigade been boldly handled. His retirement was managed with the greatest skill, and he got across the railway into the hills south of Morogoro just in time. Had he delayed the Kondoa force would have been in his way, and he would have had to fight for very existence under conditions which would have given him very little chance of getting away with an effective force. It was expected that he would at any rate fight for Morogoro, but he did not do so.

About the middle of July, when the advance down the Usambara valley took place, Tanga was occupied; and about the middle of September a combined movement by sea and land, the latter from Bagamoyo, brought about the occupation of Dar-es-Salaam without fighting.

CHAPTER IV

FROM THE CENTRAL RAILWAY TO SOUTH OF THE RUFIGI

Advance from the railway—State of troops—State of railway—End of South African brigades—Advance on Tabora—Release of civilian prisoners—Their treatment—Second division at Iringa—Break-down of their transport—Advance across Rufigi—Departure of General Smuts—Appreciation—The feeling in South Africa with regard to the campaign, and its effect.

EVERYONE hoped there would be a considerable pause in the operations as soon as our occupation of the central railway, together with Dar-es-Salaam, Tabora and the other settlements on it, was assured. The supply of Kondoa Irangi during the rainy season, and of the whole force during the advance, had been a tremendous strain on the transport. A great deal of it had been used up altogether, and the remainder needed overhaul before it could be fit for a further advance.

The health of the white troops was bad; the hospitals were full, and there were many men still on duty who ought to have been in hospital. The whole force was in great need of rest and re-equipment.

The transport had been taxed to get up supplies of food; the clothing and boots the men needed so badly it had not been possible to bring up in sufficient quantities. For a considerable time the possession of the railway gave very little relief to the transport. The enemy had done their best to make it useless to us. They had destroyed the bridges, and where these crossed deep ravines they had run trains into the gaps left by the broken bridges, filling the ravines to the level of the permanent way with wrecked rolling stock of all kinds. Serious as the damage was it was not as bad as it might have been, and as the enemy hoped and expected it would be.

When the railway had been under construction low level bridges had been used, and cuttings made in the sides of the ravines and river banks. These cuttings still existed, so that what the German engineers had done during construction our engineers could do during reconstruction. Lines could be laid along the cuttings, and low level bridges constructed of sleepers, which could be used at any rate during the dry season. The engineers said that if the enemy instead of running the railway rolling stock into the ravines had run it into the very deep cuttings, and had blown the cuttings in on top of it, the time it would have taken to make the railway of use to us would have been much longer.

There was very little rolling stock on the section of the line which came into our possession, and as a result of the advance overland to the railway. Steps were taken immediately to make this section of some use, at first, for light traffic. Motor vehicles were adapted for running on the rails, to be used as tractors for the few vans that were available. Dar-es-Salaam did not come into our possession for some time after we had arrived on the railway farther inland, and, until it did so, and the line was repaired, the railway could not be used as a line of supply. Supplies had still to be brought by the transport overland to the railway, and beyond. When the light transport on the railway could be used it relieved the transport to the extent that supplies could be brought to the nearest point, and transferred by tractor on the rails to points farther away.

The amount of rolling stock found at Dar-es-Salaam was disappointing. The majority of that which had not been destroyed was on the Tabora section, and so fell into the hands of the Belgians. The enemy had rendered this for the most part useless by removing some essential parts, but we found a good supply of these parts, and made a bargain with the Belgians. We gave them the parts in return for a proportion of the rolling stock. In a very short time trains were running right through to Tabora, and the railway took its proper place as the main line of supply for all troops on it, and based on it.

But the considerable pause that was hoped for did not come off. The enemy, who had disappeared from Morogoro to the southward without putting up the fight that was expected, was quickly followed up. There was a considerable amount of fighting in the hills south of Morogoro before the enemy was pushed into the Rufigi valley.

The troops had a bad time. The country was bare of supplies, as was always the case when we were following the German force, and the transport was stretched to the farthest limit. The effects of the climate were being felt more and more. The temporary fillip given by the forward move, which had carried the men to the central railway, had worn off. The camps along the railway were full of sick and worn-out men. There were five thousand white men in hospital and several thousand more who well might have been there.

The chief command was apparently still sanguine, still believed that the loss of the central railway and our occupation of Dar-es-Salaam and Tabora meant the end of the enemy resistance, and that, if he were given no rest, he would give in. Hence the immediate push to the Rufigi valley, where the necessity for a halt was realised.

The South African portion of the force was of no more use. The two infantry brigades were absolutely used up. The mounted troops were not so bad, but they had few horses left, and the country ahead was quite unsuited for mounted action. The other white troops were in a bad state also.

Meanwhile, the Nigerian brigade, a fine force of West Africans, had arrived, and the new King's African Rifles regiments were coming on. A new offensive was therefore planned for the closing days of the year, and an attempt was to be made to close in on the enemy on both sides of the Rufigi.

While the advance of the main force to the central railway had been in progress a combined force of British and Belgians had been moving southwards on Tabora from the Kagera River, to the west of Lake Victoria, and by the lake itself. Delays in the advance of this force had been caused by transport difficulties, and it had not been hastened by want of cordial co-operation between the two elements of the force. As a matter of fact the movement would be almost better described as the advance of two forces, to some extent in co-operation, and with a similar object.

Muanza at the southern end of the lake fell to the British force, and its capture was well managed. The enemy had made up his mind that the attack would be made from the lake by water, whereas the actual attack was delivered by land, and by a force landed some distance away. It came from an unexpected direction, and rendered the prepared defences useless.

From Muanza southward the advance was very slow, and not well co-ordinated. The enemy put up considerable resistance, especially against the Belgians. It was said that the enemy, seeing Tabora must fall, was anxious that it should fall to our troops. But our commander was unable to take advantage of the situation, and it eventually fell to a combined movement of Belgian troops from the north and from the direction of Ujiji.

This occupation resulted in the release of the civilian prisoners who had been taken in German East Africa at the beginning of the war. They had not been well treated. They had been compelled to do all sorts of menial work, including scavenging, with the obvious intention of lowering them in the eyes of the natives. The prisoners were mostly missionaries and traders, and their wives. The military prisoners were removed, and were not well treated either; the Indians and Africans being subjected, in many cases, to great brutality. Their treatment was harsh as a part of a system, the brutality was due to the class of man placed in charge of them.

The Germans were not well off for regular officers, nor had they many of the officer class. All they had they wanted with the force in the field. The result was that the men left behind in charge of prisoners were the men they could spare, and men of anything but good class. The civil prisoners were not in charge of the military chiefs but of the governor, and their treatment was undoubtedly approved of by him.

While Von Lettow, and the higher military command, can be acquitted of any intention in the matter of improper or brutal treatment of prisoners, and even of toleration of it when brought to their notice, they cannot be acquitted of neglect. That they knew the prisoners were being ill-treated is evident from the fact that they tried and punished certain men for their behaviour in this respect, but they do not appear to have taken any steps to insure better treatment by means of frequent inspections, or by appointing better-class men to take charge. One of the worst cases of brutal treatment occurred in the latter stages of the campaign.

Some of the men who had treated the prisoners badly fell into our hands, and had to answer for their crimes before a military court. One such was a native of India who had been placed in charge of Indian prisoners. He had treated them with the utmost brutality, and had been tried and given a term of imprisonment, by the German military authorities for stealing prisoners' rations. He escaped when the Belgians occupied Tabora, but was captured and handed over. He eventually faced a firing party on the shore at Dar-es-Salaam. Others were sentenced to various terms of penal servitude.

When, after the armistice, General Von Lettow came into Dar-es-Salaam, one of the first things he asked about was the fate of these men, and, on being told, expressed his full agreement with what had been done.

The Governor cannot be acquitted of intention with regard to the treatment of the civilian prisoners; treatment, in its way, morally, if not physically, as brutal as that meted out to Indians and Africans. There is very little doubt that there was deliberate intention in putting them to do tasks which would lower them in the eyes of the natives, and that such treatment was directed by the Governor.

FROM THE CENTRAL RAILWAY

In preparation for the coming attempt to round up the enemy forces, on both banks of the Rufigi, the 2nd Division was sent to Iringa. From the railway at Dodoma the supply arrangements were placed under the divisional staff, transport being allocated to it for this purpose. The task they took over was no easy one. The transport was of all sorts, heavy mechanical, light mechanical, animal and porter. The road, too, was of " all sorts," some parts fit for one sort of transport, others for another. In the dry weather there were various factors governing the sort of transport to be used; long stretches without water where mechanical transport was necessary; sandy tracts which were difficult for motors; hilly pieces where pack transport, or porters, were alone of use.

The various stretches were, of course, of different lengths. The problem to be solved, and a very difficult problem too, was how to utilise the transport available in order to get the maximum lift into Iringa. It was obviously bad management to dump fifty tons of supplies at the end of your heavy motor stretch, and only have enough light motors on the next stretch to carry forward twenty-five tons, and so on. There was no genius with the 1st Division. There was no one with any training in such a matter capable of so arranging the transport that the best possible lift was obtained. The result was that, though they were able to keep up supply, they were unable to build up any reserve of rations at Iringa. Further than this, they started building up a reserve of rations of one particular sort when it was suddenly brought home to them that they had no reserve for porters.

Orders were then at once given to send forward porter rations, and the move of these rations was in progress when down came the rain. So everything came to a standstill, and not a section could be worked except the porter stage towards the end of the road; but the porter rations had not yet got as far as that! The result, of course, was disastrous. The move had to be made with no food for the unfortunate porters, who suffered terribly, and the stoppage lasted over a fortnight.

It is difficult to blame anyone for what happened. The transport at the disposal of the division was sufficient, if used to the best advantage, to carry sufficient to build up a reserve of all sorts of rations. The division failed in two respects: they failed to make the best use of the transport, and they failed to keep a watch on the amount of each sort of ration they had in hand. The first failure was to a great extent excusable. So difficult was it to arrange the transport on this line that the experts, sent up later, required to make several trials before they were satisfied that the best use was being made of the transport. The second failure was not excusable. Someone blundered badly, and with terrible results.

At the end of the year the combined move was made, and the chief and his general staff were very sanguine, but only to be again disappointed. The crossing of the river was accomplished under the

"STUCK" ON THE ROAD TO THE RUFIGI RIVER DURING THE RAINS.
INDIAN TROOPS CROSSING LUMI RIVER DRIFT, IN THE ADVANCE ON TAVETA.

most difficult conditions, and the jaws of the pincers closed, but too late to catch the enemy between them. It was in the fighting on the Rufigi that Selous lost his life.

This was the last move made by General Smuts as Commander-in-Chief. He returned to South Africa in January, and the command passed to General Hoskins, who had come out a year earlier as Chief of the General Staff.

The fighting formations of South Africans left at the same time as General Smuts, some to be reformed for service in Europe, others to come back to East Africa after recovering their health. The climate had been too much for them. Fever and dysentery, combined with hard work and short rations, had made them totally unfit for service for some time. They were a very uneven body of men; there were men in the prime of life, but there were many boys, and many men rather old for campaigning in tropical Africa. The boys stood the hardships worst, whilst many of the older men stood them very well on the whole.

The general opinion was that the senior officers were good, but that the junior, regimental officers were incapable of looking after their men. There is no doubt that the best was not made of the rations available, nor of the food that was obtainable in the country. The excuse given by some of the officers for not having made better arrangements for the feeding of their men, when rations were short, was that the men liked best the uneconomic method of using the ration. But no proper attempts appear to have been made to make the men do anything for their own good—if the men did not like it.

That General Smuts was, and is, a very great man there is no room for doubt. There are those, however, who consider the question as to his being a great General open to argument. In considering this question it is necessary to look on the campaign from all sides, and to consider what may have been General Smuts' ideas in carrying it on as he did. How far he appears to have gained the objects he set himself to gain, and how far those which he did gain went towards the satisfactory termination of the campaign.

The actual results of General Smuts' ten months in command are plain for all to see. On his arrival the enemy was in position on the British side of the frontier between British and German East Africa, at Taveta on the slopes of Kilimanjaro. He was also on the Uganda border on the Kagera River. At General Smuts' departure all the country north of the Rufigi River was in our occupation, including, as it did, all the chief settlements. Tanga and the Usambara, Morogoro, Dar-es-Salaam, Tabora, and the whole railway system.

On the other hand, although the enemy forces were south of the Rufigi, and had been obliged to abandon the greater part of the colony, as a fighting force they were practically as strong and efficient as they had been ten months earlier. The country had been occupied, but the enemy force had not been destroyed. It cannot be said that it had even been badly defeated. It had been attacked; it had left its positions; it had retired in the face of a superior force, but it had never been soundly beaten. It had managed to avoid such a catastrophe.

For some reason or other there was a very general idea that General Smuts was averse to fighting, that he much preferred to manœuvre the enemy out of a position to driving him out, and this with the object of avoiding a fight. This seems a wrong idea altogether. General Smuts had, above all things, a logical mind. He objected to giving the enemy the advantage of fighting in a position, or on ground, chosen by himself. His idea was plainly to use his superior strength to make the enemy leave his chosen position; to manœuvre him out of it, in fact, and then to use his mounted troops to intercept and force him to fight on ground of his, General Smuts', choosing.

It was not the fault of General Smuts that the enemy was never placed in such a position that he would have to fight a general action to free himself, and, moreover, fight it under circumstances decidedly unpleasant for him. General Smuts' plans, on several occasions, would have resulted in placing the enemy in such a situation had it not been for the want of enterprise, to call it by no harder name, on the part of his mounted brigade commanders.

South Africa did not, at first, take the campaign in East Africa very seriously. Neither the people as a whole, nor the men who came up to take part in it.

They did not expect a long campaign as far as fighting was concerned. They thought they would have a walk' over; that in a few weeks, or, at the worst, a few months, they would be back in their homes. There was a general idea that the object for which they were fighting was not worth the loss of South African lives.

The subordinate commanders, in a considerable number of cases, felt that, under the circumstances, they were not justified in taking any action which might involve any considerable number of casualties. In the first place they agreed with the opinion that the object was not worth the loss of lives, in the second they thought that the feeling in South Africa was so strong on this point that they would be ostracised, both socially and politically, if they became responsible for any action resulting in such.

Opportunities were let slip which, if taken advantage of, would, almost certainly, have resulted in the serious crippling, if not in the actual destruction, of the enemy force. As it was, Von Lettow was now south of the Rufigi with a force practically as strong as it had ever been. The fact that the commanders responsible were not at once sent back to South Africa caused much comment on the part of that portion of the force that did not come from South Africa.

CHAPTER V

PREPARATIONS FOR NEW CAMPAIGN

Unpleasant position for new Commander-in-Chief—State of the force—Efforts to get transport—Importance of maintaining hold on country occupied—Bases and lines of supply during rainy season—The Wintgens raid—Programme for new campaign—The supply of porters—Appointment of General Van Deventer to chief command of force—Suggested reasons for change.

THE new Commander-in-Chief was in a very unpleasant position. General Smuts stated publicly that the campaign in East Africa was over, and that all that now remained to be done was to sweep up the remnants of the enemy force. He implied thereby that his operations during the past nine months had not only resulted in the occupation of all the enemy territory north of the Rufigi, but in the virtual destruction of his force. The authorities at home, and elsewhere, were inclined, rather naturally perhaps, to accept this view of the situation. They evidently expected that General Hoskins would be able to report within a few weeks that the enemy-force had ceased to exist. They also appeared to think that that force was reduced to a few scattered parties of demoralised askaris, only waiting for a chance to give themselves up, and that their leaders were of the same mind. Nothing could have been farther from the truth. The enemy-force was compact, their morale good, and the leaders as determined as ever on resistance to the end.

General Hoskins, the man on the spot, looked on the situation with a very different eye. He was sure that there was another and a very strenuous campaign ahead; an anticipation which was amply justified by events. His efforts to convince the Home Authorities of this fact were not altogether successful. They seemed to think that he should take immediate steps to bring matters to an end. They did not seem to realise a situation which was obvious to the Commander-in-Chief, and everyone else on the spot, namely that, at the moment, neither as regards troops nor transport was the Commander-in-Chief in a position to carry on a campaign of any sort. Further, the rainy season was again coming on, and, in the area in which operations would have to be undertaken, operations were impossible at that time of the year. The troops had been very hard worked during the advance from the frontier to the Rufigi; a distance, as the crow flies, of over two hundred miles. They had had no rest to speak of. They had been badly fed, and had suffered from want of all comforts owing to absence of clothing and equipment. They had been operating in areas regarded as being among the most unhealthy in that country of unhealthy areas, German East Africa. The transport was used up; the mechanical transport

PREPARATIONS FOR CAMPAIGN

broken down, and in need of thorough overhaul and reconditioning; the animal transport mostly dead, and the porters worn out and debilitated. It can safely be said that there was scarcely a man, white or black, taking part in this advance who had escaped several bouts of fever of a bad stamp. The enemy forces were south of the Rufigi, in the Mahenge and Liwale areas, and farther to the south-west in the area about Songea and Tunduru. Our troops had followed them up in their retirement, and were also south of the river, occupying the angle between the sea as far south as Kilwa, and the Rufigi as far west as Utete. Farther west the Nigerians were at Mpangwas, almost due south of Mikesse on the central railway; and farther west again there was a detached force at Iringa. Lindi on the coast, south of Kilwa, was occupied, and the Nyasaland force was holding the south-west corner of German territory in the neighbourhood of Songea. In every area the troops were in touch with the enemy.

From a political, as well as from a military, point of view it was most important that the country north of the Rufigi, which had been occupied, and was being administered by us, should be denied to the enemy. To effect this it was necessary that the troops should stay pretty much where they were; neither could they be moved into more healthy areas, nor to places to which supply would be easy.

The base lines of supply were the central railway, the Rufigi delta, and the sea. From the central railway lines had to be maintained to Iringa and Mpangwas, in both cases across a big river, which, even in the dry season, was a formidable obstacle. The difficulties of making good use of transport on the Dodoma-Iringa line have been mentioned in a former chapter. The transport experts had so far overcome these difficulties that a good lift was being obtained, but this could not be expected to continue when the rains began. It was known that the Germans considered the road impracticable for the four wet months of the year. The Ruaha drains a very large area, is a very formidable obstacle at all times, and, in the rains, and for a considerable part of its course, overflows its banks, and floods the country on each side for several miles. Where the road crosses it the width of the valley under water is about sixteen miles.

There was not sufficient transport available to get in supplies to last the garrison through the rains. Boats fitted with motors were got ready at Dar-es-Salaam, with the idea of maintaining a ferry, and so keeping the road open. But though they went very well in the harbour, and experts thought there was no doubt that they would do what was wanted, it was found, when, with great trouble, they were got on to the river, that they were quite unable to act in the strong current they encountered, and, but for a fortunate discovery, things would have been desperate.

When the books of a flour mill at Kilossa were being examined a return showing the receipts of grain during 1916 was found. Among the entries were receipts of grain from Iringa all through the rains, the grain being shown as received in porter loads. This made it evident that communication was possible. Further investigation showed that there was a direct path from Kilossa to Iringa, which crossed the Ruaha at a place where the river was confined between high banks, and which prevented it spreading over the surrounding country as it did on the Dodoma road. But this road had its drawbacks as for only a very short distance at either end could any wheeled transport be used, whilst for the greater part of the way it was impracticable for anything but porters, excepting a short stretch fit for donkeys. So that whilst a certain amount was sent over the Dodoma road, and ferried across the river in native boats, by using the Kilossa path as well it was possible to keep up a sufficient supply for the garrison throughout the wet season. There were times of anxiety, but, taking it altogether, this road caused less trouble than any of the other transport lines.

The line from Mikesse to Mpangwas was a nightmare. It had been impossible to get any reserve forward on this line. For some distance out to Mikesse light motor transport was used, but the road was over very bad country, and newly made, consequently there were frequent breaks. In the Rufigi valley nothing but porter transport was possible, and even that was appallingly difficult. The road ran for many miles through sticky mud, and water so deep that the porters were working for whole marches up to their armpits.

The wastage was dreadful. The motor drivers lasted a few weeks at the outside. As for the porters, they went sick and died at an alarming rate. Some sort of supply was kept up to the troops in front, but not more than just sufficient to keep them going. On many days only half rations reached them, on some days it was less.

The officer commanding complained—he had good cause—that his men were being starved, and that his officers could not go on unless they had some comforts sent up to them. His messages became more and more abrupt, till they might have been regarded as rude. When the weather improved, and the road was considered to be quite passable, he came back over it to Dar-es-Salaam, so was able to judge what the difficulties had been for himself. In fact, even then he found it sufficiently formidable. On arrival at G.H.Q. he went round all the offices he had bombarded with his complaints, and asked to be allowed to withdraw everything he had said. He declared that now that he had seen the road his only wonder was that anything at all had been got up.

It had been hoped that it would have been possible to use the river, above the estuary, for the supply of troops within reach of it, but no steamers strong enough to work against the current were to be had. The estuary itself was used for the supply to the troops in the northern part of the triangle,

PREPARATIONS FOR CAMPAIGN

through Mohoro and, at first, through Utete. Here also things did not go really well.

Mohoro was not on the banks of the main river, but a short distance up a tributary flowing in from the south. This tributary became impossible, the stream being so strong that the steamers could make no way against it. By establishing a line of porter-transport across the triangle between the two rivers supply was kept up for a time, but the water overflowed on to the triangle, and filled hollows in the road to such an extent as to prevent the porters getting across. It was only after very heavy work that boats could be conveyed from the river to this flooded area, and communication restored just in time to save the situation.

The I.G.C. and his staff were having an anxious time, for as soon as one line was restored another came to a standstill. The line inland from Kilwa was giving trouble; the troops in the triangle were moving southwards and coming on to this line for supply; the animal transport, which had been used there, was dying, and there were no porters to take its place. The only line that gave little or no trouble was Lindi. There the troops were all close to the port at the time in question.

But it was a very anxious time for everyone connected with supply. On every line it had to be done from hand to mouth. There had been no time to build up reserves before the rains broke. Where motor transport was in use there were daily reports of breaks in the roads, and daily reports of shortage of cars and drivers owing to accidents and sickness. Where animals were used the numbers dwindled with great rapidity; mules and donkeys alike were dying of fly. As for porters, the daily death and sick reports were very alarming, and there were no reserves. Every useful car, every useful driver, had to be " dug out " and sent on to one or other of the lines. The remount lines were empty of animals fit for work, and the porter lines quite empty.

Porters were the urgent need at this time, and every effort was made to get them. Batches came in slowly, and many of these were delayed by outbreaks of disease which necessitated their being kept in quarantine camp for a long time. As they came in they were hastily equipped and sent to that line which seemed, for the moment, in most serious danger of breaking down. No proper pool of men could be formed from which those best suited to a particular sort of country could be selected for work there. The need of the moment had to be met from the first lot of men that came to hand, and, in consequence, men who ought to have been sent to the coast had to be sent up country, and vice versâ, much to the detriment of their health. Starvation was averted, more cannot be said. The men in the field received a bare sufficiency, the supply of comforts was impossible. They suffered great hardships having to live like this at the worst time of the year, and in, possibly, the worst climate in the world.

Just at this time, when every nerve was strained to

keep up the supply to the troops south of the Rufigi, there came news of a very unwelcome development. Major Wintgens, with about six hundred men detached from the main enemy force, after being engaged with a portion of the Nyasaland force in the Songea area, had broken away towards the north, with the avowed intention at attacking Tabora.

He was followed up by a detachment of the Nyasaland force, who had, however, very little chance of stopping him. He moved at a good pace, clearing the country of all supplies as he went, and making it imperative that the pursuing force should be supplied from the rear. It was, in consequence, not long before they were brought to a standstill for want of food.

A regiment composed of ex-German askaris, who had taken service with us after capture, was sent to the north-west of Iringa to watch the country, and, if possible, delay his movements until a force could be got together to intercept him. This was soon got ready and sent up, and the Belgians were asked to co-operate by sending some troops, which they did.

Wintgens had a choice of many roads, and was in a part of the country where concealment of movement was easy. He managed to elude our troops, crossed the railway, and proceeded in the direction of Muanza. A Nigerian battalion came up with him, but too late in the day to do much. He proceeded to Ikoma, where he took up a position in which he was attacked by the Belgians, who were rather badly mauled. He then went off to the west followed by the Belgians, but not very closely. He found the road into British East Africa, in the neighbourhood of Magadi, closed by King's African Rifles and so went off towards Aruscha, which he found in occupation of the Cape Corps. He then turned towards the Tanga railway, held up a train at Sami, and captured two officers. Then turning south again he made his way to the neighbourhood of Mpapua, and, after a wandering career of several months' duration, was at last compelled to lay down his arms.

Wintgens himself had surrendered when his force crossed the central railway on its way north, and the force had from that point been commanded by a man named Naumann.

They had both done their job, and had done it well. For months a considerable number of troops had been engaged in following them, and trying to intercept them. Troops that were wanted elsewhere, and many times the number of this enemy detachment. They had made us use transport for the supply of these troops which was very badly wanted elsewhere. They had also upset the whole country through which they passed.

Meanwhile, in addition to the maintenance of the troops in the field, preparations had to be made for the new campaign south of the Rufigi, which would have to be undertaken as soon as the country dried up sufficiently. The lines on which the Chief

MOTOR TRANSPORT ON BLACK COTTON SOIL DURING THE RAINS.
LABOUR CORPS. AN AMMUNITION COLUMN.

PREPARATIONS FOR CAMPAIGN

decided to work were to lay a light railway as far as possible inland from Kilwa, use light motor transport from rail-head, and porters to give the columns a radius of action in country where the absence of roads of any sort precluded the use of motors. As to light railway material, there was a certain amount of track which had been used for plantation work, and some which had been in use at Handeni. South Africa was also able to supply some. The shops at Dar-es-Salaam were available to convert motor-cars to serve as tractors on the railway.

The construction of the track was energetically taken in hand by the railway department, and very good progress was made in spite of the drawbacks of bad weather and bad climate. The War Office was urged to supply the light motors required for use beyond rail-head, and, when it at last realised the need, managed, in spite of world shortage due to the great numbers required for other theatres, to arrange a supply, from America, of some very efficient cars. South Africa and India were called on, and a good many cars were obtained from those two countries; some being fitted with transport bodies in the workshops there, others being sent as they were, and fitted up in the shops at Dar-es-Salaam.

The porter-supply question was the one that really caused most anxiety. Up to that time British East Africa had supplied the great majority of the porters, but now it seemed as if that source of supply was giving out. So, realising the extreme urgency of keeping up a supply, the Acting Governor took special steps to assist the Commander-in-Chief. He placed the services of a high official of the Protectorate at the disposal of the force. This official took charge of the supply, made all arrangements for recruiting, and, at the same time, looked after the welfare of the men recruited. The result was very satisfactory, for large numbers were then forthcoming.

But these demands were so large that there was no prospect of getting the full number from this source. All that could be hoped for was that the wastage, which was alarming, could be made good. Other sources of supply had therefore to be tapped. West Africa responded to a request for help, and recruiting was started all along the west coast. A considerable number of excellent carriers were sent under their own officers, officials for the most part of the various administrations in that part of the world. Many more would have been sent had it not been for the difficulty of providing shipping.

German East Africa provided a large number, but a great many tribes in that part are nearly useless as carriers. Attempts were made to get labour from Portuguese East Africa, but without marked success. There are any number of excellent men to be had in that country, for it is from there that comes a great deal of the labour used in the mines on the Rand. The organisation providing that labour undertook to get men for the force—for

PREPARATIONS FOR CAMPAIGN

a consideration—and they did produce a few men—at a price. Direct recruitment in other areas, though authorised by the superior Portuguese authorities, was successfully thwarted by the minor officials of the companies " farming " the various parts of the country.

By the middle of May things were looking a little brighter. The new arrangements in British East Africa were bringing in a fair number of men; the West Africans had started on their way; German East was providing its quotâ. Cars were coming in from England, America, India and South Africa. The light railway was getting on. Above all, the rains were coming to an end without there having been any actual failure of supply. Fresh troops were arriving from India to replace those which had been a long time in the country, and had suffered badly from the climate. New King's African Rifle Regiments were coming to hand. In fact, everything was getting ready for a move as soon as the country should have sufficiently dried up.

At this juncture the Home Government thought fit to remove General Hoskins and put in his place General Van Deventer from South Africa. General Hoskins was thus deprived of a chance of using the instrument he had made. It was really a new instrument.

In January he had taken over from General Smuts an instrument—however good its material—blunted and useless for any offensive action. A force tired in body and mind, and without transport. Everything moral and material had been expended in reaching the Rufigi. As a defensive force it still had value, as an offensive force none. It required rest, reinforcement and re-equipment. During his four months in command General Hoskins had restored that force. In spite of the inevitable loss of interest on the part of all upon whom he was dependent for the supply of men and material, due to General Smuts' ill-timed declaration that the campaign was over, he had managed to get things done by urgent representations and hard work.

It so happened that this four months coincided with that period of the year when campaigning in tropical Africa is impossible. He had utilised this time of enforced abstention from active operations to the best advantage. He was, therefore, able to hand over to his successor a new-made instrument, sharp and ready for immediate use. Needless to say he had the fullest sympathy of the whole force in what could not have been other than a bitter disappointment.

The reasons for the change were obscure. The Home Authorities were supposed to have been dissatisfied because more had not been done in the time; more active operations undertaken. But this can scarcely have been the case, as, presumably, they knew something of the conditions in the country during the rainy season, even if they did not fully appreciate the condition to which the force had been reduced by the operations of the previous year.

It was suggested, as an explanation, that the

military authorities at home, men who could understand and appreciate the difficulties of the country and the situation generally, had themselves no say in the change, and that it was made entirely for political reasons. This seems a more probable explanation—that it was the work of the politicians, and that the War Office was merely the conveyer of the order.

Surely it can only have been so, for such an action might well seem as nothing to the politician when out to please one of their own kind, though a grave injustice to a regular soldier.

CHAPTER VI

FROM THE RUFIGI TO THE ROVUMA

Arrival of General Van Deventer—Plans for campaign—Probable object of enemy—Reasons for above opinion—The native African soldier—The moves from Kilwa and Lindi—The fight at Mahiwa—Retirement of the enemy, over the Rovuma, into Portuguese territory—Surrender of Mahenge and part of enemy—The Portuguese attitude—The airship—Suggested reason for Von Lettow's hard fighting.

GENERAL VAN DEVENTER arrived towards the end of May to take over the command of the force. As Commander of the 2nd Division, under General Smuts, he had been in command at Kondoa Iranga; in the advance from that place to the central railway, eastwards down the railway, and later on at Iringa. He had returned sick to the Union at about the same time as General Smuts. He was, therefore, no stranger to the country and its conditions. The general impression he had given was that of a very capable commander in the field from a fighting point of view, but rather neglectful on the administrative side. When in command of a division his staff had been almost entirely composed of men belonging to the South African forces, whose knowledge of administration was not conspicuous.

On first arrival he was very shy of talking English,

and all business with his English speaking staff had to be carried on through an interpreter. He was very anxious to make a start with active operations,[1] but, before taking any steps, or making any plans, he visited the forces in the Kilwa and Lindi areas to see for himself how far the preparations had gone.

The next move would obviously be an advance inland from the coast to get at the enemy, and the question to be settled was as to whether this advance could be most effectively made from Kilwa or Lindi, or should it be a combined advance from both places?

The position the enemy would be in by the time matters were ready for an advance was a matter for speculation. There were strong indications of an intention to move off southwards, possibly across the Rovuma into Portuguese territory. If the enemy did move to the south it meant that Lindi would become the principal, advanced sea-base in place of Kilwa. The prospect of having to use Lindi on a large scale was not pleasing. A good many of the ships working on the coast, including most of the hospital ships, could not use Lindi harbour. Lindi itself was not a suitable starting place for the light railway which would have to be constructed. Mingoyo, eleven miles up the river, was obviously the place from which this would actually have to start, and everything would have to be taken up there in lighters. The sequence of supply would thus be by sea to Lindi, by lighter from Lindi to Mingoyo, thence by light railway to rail-head, then by light car as far as roads would allow, and finally by porter to the troops off the road.

Our only object now was the destruction of the enemy force. By far the greater part, and by far the most important part, of German East Africa was effectively in our occupation. We had, therefore, to prevent the enemy returning to that part; to engage him, and destroy him, in the country between the Rufigi and the Rovuma.

As has already been said there were good reasons for thinking that Von Lettow would move off to the south—into Portuguese East Africa. His only reason for remaining where he was would be the sentimental one of wishing to continue to hold a piece of what had been German territory, and possibly a thought that if peace should come in Europe he would have a better position, as a force still in being, in the colony. Against remaining was the fact that food supplies in that part of the country were very short indeed. The whole country had been eaten out so completely that the natives had practically no seed grain left. South of the Rovuma, once over the foodless tract, and just south of the river, supplies were to be had in abundance.

Nor was it only foodstuffs that would be available, for there was every prospect of being able to get warlike stores in the way of rifles, ammunition, light artillery and machine-guns; the Portuguese being, as Von Lettow very well knew, incapable of offering any sort of effective resistance. He was very well aware, too, that we could not leave our allies to be over-run by his force, and, therefore, that his movement into Portuguese territory would not result in the troops of the East African Force being released for service elsewhere.

The way was open. In every direction, excepting to the south, he was faced by our troops. Assuming that his object was to occupy our troops in East Africa as long as possible, and at the same time make it necessary for us to keep a large force there, it was justifiable to think that he would choose the easiest road, and not take the risk of very materially reducing his effective force by fighting.

Meanwhile, whatever his intentions were, he remained in touch with our forces both in the Kilwa and Lindi areas, and in considerable strength. A combined advance for both bases therefore seemed to offer the best chance in dealing effectively with him. If we could drive him away from the Kilwa area, compel him to move to the south, and, at the same time, intercept his move by an advance of the Lindi force, he would have to fight practically the whole available strength we had in East Africa.

At first Lindi had been occupied very lightly. Just a garrison to hold the port, and not strong enough to attempt to clear the enemy away from the immediate neighbourhood, or to allow the commencement of a light railway which would certainly be needed. More troops were therefore sent to strengthen the force sufficiently for such an operation. The strengthened force made several attempts to drive the enemy away without success, but eventually succeeded in manœuvring him out of his positions.

The force at Kilwa was also not, at first, strong enough to attempt a regular advance, but it was in contact with the enemy, and there was a considerable amount of fighting, though not on a very large scale, and not invariably resulting in our favour.

By this time the German askari had become very good indeed, especially as a fighter in the bush, whilst we were relying more and more upon newly raised battalions of the King's African Rifles.

It takes a long time to turn an African savage into a reliable soldier. The African is by no means wanting in intelligence, nor is he wanting in courage, but when first enlisted he is very much " all abroad." Everything is so utterly strange to him. His intelligence wants training before his training as a soldier can be begun. The old King's African Rifles battalions were a long-service force; the men were mostly old soldiers, and first class fighting troops. The number of recruits in the ranks was very small. In raising the new battalions a small nucleus of old soldiers was transferred from an old battalion, and a battalion of recruits built up on them. This of course meant that the old battalions suffered by losing a proportion of their old and reliable men.

It was impossible to give the new battalions as much training as they ought to have had, from the fact that they were wanted in the field. A great deal depended on their introduction to fighting. If blooded gently, and successful in their first fight, the chances of a battalion turning out well were very good. If, on the other hand, they were badly knocked about the first time they went into action it might, and probably would, be a long time before they could be relied on. Unfortunately, in a few cases, new battalions were tried too high at first, and some never recovered from the experience.

When the state of the country admitted of a move it soon became plain that Von Lettow did not intend retiring to the Rovuma without fighting, and up to the middle of August very little progress was made.

Our casualties in action, combined with sickness as a result of being in the unhealthy Kilwa area during the rains, had reduced the effective strength very materially, and, until reinforcements arrived from India, the Nigerians could be got down, and all put in at Kilwa, no real advance was possible. As Von Lettow had not moved off south it was now thought that he would hang on to the Mahenge area, and intended to fight it out there. There was some fighting south-east of Iringa in which the Belgians took part, and in which the enemy retired on Mahenge.

The advance from both Kilwa and Lindi was strongly opposed by the enemy. The Kilwa force made the most rapid progress, and, after several fights in which both sides suffered severe casualties, the enemy retired towards the south. The Nigerians managed to fall on the main enemy force on the move, and, though unable to stop the movement, handled him very severely.

It then seemed that Von Lettow had made up his mind that he could do nothing effective with the Kilwa force, and intended to try what he could do elsewhere. At first it looked as though he meant going to Tunduru, and attacking the Nyasaland force in that and the Songea districts. If he ever did mean this he soon changed his mind, for he turned on the Lindi force, now considerably strengthened and advancing along the Lindi-Massassi road. The Nigerian Brigade was detached from the Kilwa force and sent by a bad road to reinforce the Lindi force. They had many difficulties. One battalion got detached, and had some difficulty in getting round the flank of the German force, by a night march, to join up. They reached the Lindi force just as the enemy attack commenced, were placed in reserve some miles behind the fighting line, to recover from the march, and without any food. They were naturally, and for the time being, rather knocked up.

Great things were hoped for from this fight, and justifiably so. The Lindi force was fairly strong in itself, and with the Nigerian Brigade added there was very good ground for thinking it strong enough to decisively defeat Von Lettow. In order to complete his discomfiture two other columns were moved down from the Kilwa area by roads farther inland than that followed by the Nigerians. These columns were to be ready to fall on the enemy's

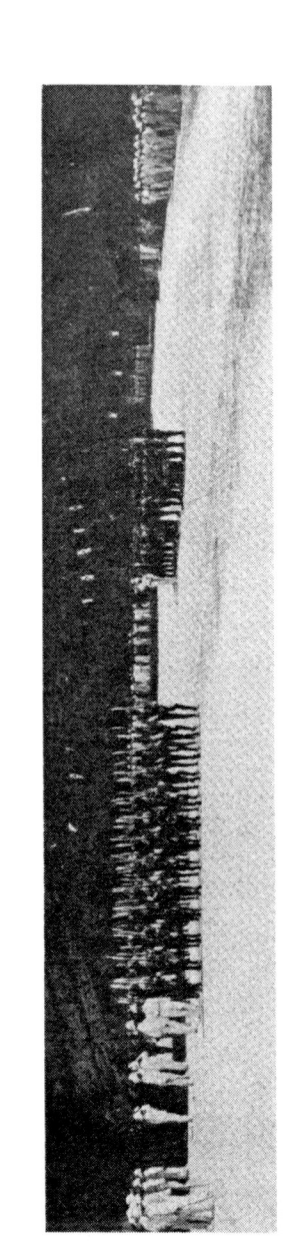

THE KAISER'S BIRTHDAY. REVIEW OF GERMAN NATIVE TROOPS AT DAR-ES-SALAAM.
A GERMAN ASKARI BATTALION ON THE MARCH.
(From photographs found after the occupation of Dar-es-Salaam.)

flank and rear when he had been driven westward or southward by the Lindi force.

Unfortunately the move was not successful. After a three days' action the officer commanding our force withdrew from the ground on which he had been fighting. The enemy remained in his position. The Nigerians were considered, by the officer commanding the Lindi force, not fit to be put into the fight. Had they arrived in good condition, or had they had time to recover and take part, they would, almost certainly, have turned what was more or less a drawn fight into a decisive success. In fact, the fight was so even that it is possible their entry, even in the condition they then were, would have tipped the scale.

The casualties in the three days' fighting were very severe; so severe that the force was in no condition to renew the fight until it could be made good, and as Von Lettow also made no attempt to renew it, it may be assumed that he had suffered in proportion.

After some days the enemy disappeared in a south-westerly direction. The Lindi force then advanced, and came in contact with a part of the enemy force away to the left of the road. Here there was a sharp fight. The enemy continued their movement, skilfully covering themselves with rear-guard, and then disappeared into the bush. The columns that had come down from Kilwa joined in, but the enemy was now well away, and was never again brought to serious action.

Touch was regained by a cavalry patrol, but by that time he was close down to the Rovuma, which he crossed, and into Portuguese territory, in the last days of November. So, for a time, it was doubtful where the enemy had gone, and several weeks elapsed before we were in touch with him again.

When Von Lettow moved against the Kilwa force he left a strong detachment, under one of his best officers, in the Mahenge area. On deciding to move south into Portuguese territory he sent orders to this force to meet him on the Rovuma. A force of King's African Rifles coming from the west fell in with this force on its march, and, though not strong enough to stop the movement, they engaged and succeeded in delaying it. The German commander was now out of touch with Von Lettow, and had no idea as to current happenings, for, instead of finding the main German force where he had expected it to be, he found himself in the midst of our columns. He then tried to get out, but, finding himself opposed in whatever direction he took, surrendered with his whole force, three hundred Europeans, one thousand five hundred askaris, and many followers, including a very large number of women belonging to the troops.

When Von Lettow left the Lindi district he only took with him into Portuguese East Africa the fit men of his force; about two hundred Europeans and one thousand five hundred askaris. The sick, and all superfluous civilians, were left behind.

The ex-Governor, Von Schnee, he took with him.

The Portuguese expressed themselves as confident of their ability to stop the enemy on the Rovuma. They had a post of about a thousand men at Ngomano. But a few shots from the enemy were sufficient to bring about the surrender of this post, and Von Lettow was able to re-equip his force with new rifles, and replenish his stock of ammunition.

It was at this period that news reached us of a German airship. This was supposed to be on its way to East Africa from some point in south-east Europe, and intended to land somewhere in the neighbourhood of Liwale, west of Lindi. This seemed an extraordinary enterprise in view of the long journey, and there was much speculation as to the object. Was it to bring something of which Von Lettow was much in need, or was it to take him and the Governor away?

It seemed possible that the expected arrival of this airship may have had a great deal to do with the vigorous fight Von Lettow put up in the Kilwa and Lindi districts. He cannot have had any hope of gaining a real material advantage, of destroying the force opposed to him, by this departure from his usual methods of warfare. The forces he had acted against were not detachments that he had hoped to wipe out. There must have been some strong reason for such a display of fighting energy, and the airship may have been the reason.

CHAPTER VII

THE CAMPAIGN IN PORTUGUESE EAST AFRICA

Orders to carry on campaign—Only African troops to remain—Commander-in-Chief's forecast of possible course of campaign—Plans—Tactics—Reason for retention of senior officer as Commander-in-Chief—Portuguese troops—Port Amelia—Minor Portuguese officials—The natives of Portuguese East Africa—Advance inland from Port Amelia—Mozambique—Quelimane—Return of enemy northwards—Recrossing of Rovuma—Preparations to meet new situation—The Armistice—Von Lettow and Schnee in Dar-es-Salaam—The end of the East African force—Departure of General Van Deventer—An appreciation.

IT was in the last week of November that Von Lettow, with his band of faithful veterans, disappeared into the sparsely inhabited, almost barren tract, of country south of the Rovuma. This meant that German East Africa was clear of enemy troops, but it did not mean that the task of the East African Force was at an end. The enemy force was in the territory of an ally totally unable to protect his territory, or to prevent it being pillaged and over-run from end to end.

As long as it was not certain that Von Lettow would succeed in reaching their boundary, supposing his intention was to go south, the Portuguese expressed absolute confidence in their ability to stop him at the river. But when it became plain that he was going that way, and there was nothing to stop him doing so, they began to call very urgently for assistance. The Home Authorities made it plain that the East African Force was not to content itself with taking measures to prevent the return of the enemy to German East Africa, but was, in conjunction with the Portuguese, to follow up the remnant of the enemy force and destroy it, or force its surrender.

The new campaign was to be carried on with African troops. The Indian regiments and the Nigerian brigade were to return to India and Nigeria, to be brought up to strength, and prepared for service in some other theatre of war. The remnants of the white regiments were to be sent away. Only the King's African Rifles and the Gold Coast regiment were to remain; the latter only temporarily.

It may seem that it ought to have been a simple matter to bring to account a force of two hundred whites and fifteen hundred blacks, but, in reality, the circumstances of the case made it anything but easy. The men with Von Lettow were veterans. In bush-fighting very decidedly better, man for man, than any we could put against them. The country in which the campaign was to be carried on is a very large one; a great extent of it covered with thick bush, in which two forces can easily be within a few miles of one another without either being aware of the other's presence. In this bush it is an easy matter for a small force to hold up for hours a very much superior force by the use of skilfully placed rear-guards with machine-guns; a form of warfare in which the enemy were particularly efficient. Various opinions were held by men of experience in East African fighting as to the advantage the defensive had in the bush; no one, however, put that advantage as low as three to one in its favour.

In forming a plan of campaign to bring the enemy to book it was very necessary to estimate what the plans of the enemy commander were likely to be. The personal estimate of the Commander-in-Chief was that Von Lettow would keep on the move in the areas where food was available, and avoid anything like a general action, by the skilful use of rear-guards, until the ripening of the crops in German East Africa made a return to that country possible, when he would try to get back into the Songea district and work up north. So following much the same line as Wintgens had followed in his raid. The Commander-in-Chief went so far as to point out on the map the place where he expected Von Lettow would try to cross the Rovuma, if he escaped our columns. The place so indicated was within a very few miles of the point at which he actually did cross the river some ten months after that forecast had been made.

This estimate of the Commander-in-Chief was based on sound considerations, and the event proved their accuracy. In spite of all arguments in favour of the view that Von Lettow must have definitely abandoned German East Africa, and had no intention of returning, the Commander-in-Chief stuck to his opinion that the move into Portuguese territory was only temporary, and was undertaken because of the difficulty of feeding troops north of the Rovuma.

In Portuguese territory Von Lettow lost his standing as a representative of the German government on German territory, and that he would be content to give that up the Commander-in-Chief considered very unlikely. The ground for believing that, if he did manage to return, he would cross the river near Songea was that, by coming north in that area, he would have a narrower foodless belt to cross than farther east. That he would keep to the food areas was obvious, but it was also possible to see that he would keep to them in the centre of the country, as, by so doing, he increased our difficulties in getting at him; for, in the centre of the country, he was some two hundred miles away from our bases.

It was plain that, in order to bring the enemy to book, it would be necessary to engage him with decidedly superior forces, and that the best chance of forcing an issue was by the combined movement of converging columns. A single force coming up with him would certainly be held off by the skilful use of rear-guards for sufficient time to allow of the main body escaping under cover of darkness, and disappearing into the bush. There was no reason to suppose that Von Lettow would depart in any way from his usual procedure, namely, to avoid any action with a force strong enough to do him material damage, yet taking every opportunity offered of destroying small detachments.

It was important that every column used in converging movements should be strong enough to hold its own until given time for other forces in that area to get up and join in the fight. It was necessary, in this connection, not to lose sight of the fact that communication in the bush is at no time easy to maintain, and often impossible.

At first everyone expected that the rank of Commander-in-Chief would be done away with, and someone of lower rank, probably General Northey, put in charge of operations. The force was now so reduced in numbers that it seemed scarcely a command for a lieutenant-general. But no such step was taken, it may be assumed because, by an old treaty, whenever British and Portuguese troops act together they shall act as one force under the command of the senior officer, whichever army he belongs to, and it was not desired that any risks should be run of that senior officer being other than British.

The Portuguese troops were no match for the German askaris. Any encounter between them meant a distinct gain to the enemy in the way of arms, ammunition and supplies of all sorts, at a minimum of cost. The protection of Portuguese centres, and all operations against the enemy, under these circumstances must fall to us. It was also of direct importance to us that the enemy should not attack the Portuguese, or come in contact with them, considering that such contact meant getting supplies of which he was so much in need.

To follow the enemy into the barren country south of the Rovuma was useless, so further touch was lost for a time. Only vague reports as to the route he had taken being received from scouts and from Portuguese sources. It seemed that he was likely to go westwards rather than south, but news was sure to come of his movements as soon as he got into the more thickly populated areas for which he must be making in order to get food. The interval was not unwelcome as there were gaps to be filled in our battalions, and new arrangements to be made.

It was not very long before news came that the enemy was on the road towards Port Amelia. The Portuguese became very nervous. To safeguard Port Amelia a small force was landed there, and orders were given for the Gold Coast Regiment to be sent to make everything sure. Some excitement was caused by the ship on which this regiment was being carried, from Lindi, running ashore off Mikandani, and remaining fixed. The question then asked was, who will get to Port Amelia first, the Germans or the Gold Coast Regiment? In the long run the Gold Coast Regiment arrived in time to make the German detachment think better of their intended raid.

It soon became certain that the main force of the enemy was in the Medo area, due west of Port Amelia, which now became a main base for our operations in Portuguese territory. As a base it was not all that might have been wished. Port Amelia itself is not at the end of the road leading inland to Medo and beyond; the end of the road is at Bandari, eight miles across the bay. All stores had therefore to be taken to Bandari in native dhows, and landed on an open beach, which, under certain conditions, is sometimes unusable for days at a time. As everything has to be landed by hand, and carried from stranded boats over a long stretch of sand, the amount it was possible to land there in twenty-four hours was limited. The road was not an easy one to arrange. There were stretches of black cotton soil over which motor transport was quite impossible in wet weather. These it would be necessary to bridge with porter transport as soon as the rains began, and they might begin at any time.

The difficulty came in this way, if porter transport had to be used to any considerable extent it would be impossible to land sufficient food at Bandari for both porters and troops. As long as the road could carry motor transport it was possible to feed the troops ahead. There was, therefore, only one thing that could save the situation, and that was the possibility of buying food in the districts ahead. On that we had to gamble.

Luckily, before the necessity for using large numbers of porters arose, food was available, and the special officers sent out managed to get in sufficient to make up deficiencies.

The minor Portuguese officials were very annoying. The various parts of the country are leased to companies whose only form of activity appears to be the collection of taxes from the natives. The minor officials are really the servants of the companies, not of the Portuguese government. The natives were ready enough to come to us and serve as porters, and bring in food as soon as they found we were going to pay them—a thing the Portuguese never did—but the minor officials did not approve of this for their own reasons.

To save trouble we undertook to pay the hut tax for the men who came to us, which did not suit the minor officials at all, because, when they collected the tax, they got considerably more than the legitimate amount out of the unfortunate native, and put the extra into their own pockets. They, therefore, used every means in their power to make it difficult for us to get men. They carried off the wives of the men who came, on the pretence that the hut tax had not been paid. They even went so far as to interfere with the men we sent out to get labour, not even stopping short of murder.

Remonstrances to the government of the company brought assurances that orders had been issued to stop all this sort of activity, and to give us help; but the orders, if sent, had very little effect, and it was only when we took matters into our own hands, and showed the underlings that we intended to take very drastic steps with them, that we were able to get men. Later on, when we left the country, they had their revenge on the men who had helped us, for several of these head-men were murdered.

The natives, one and all, hated the Portuguese with a bitter hatred, and in many parts were in open rebellion against them. They were willing to help anyone who was against their hated masters. They did not understand the situation. They knew that the Germans were enemies of the Portuguese, and so, naturally, were anxious to help them. They did not understand our position at all, but thought we were going to oust the Portuguese, and so were equally ready to help us. They were ready to give information, but, as they could not distinguish between the two forces, their information of the presence of an enemy-force at a certain place could only be taken to mean that there were some troops there.

The force put in from Port Amelia met the enemy on the road to Medo, pushed him back beyond that place, and followed him up to the south-west. A combined movement by this column, divided into two parts, and a column of troops from the Nyasaland side—by which it was hoped to surround the enemy—failed, partly owing to difficulties of ground, and partly owing to difficulties of communication between the different parts of the force, but chiefly owing to a mistake as to the actual position of the enemy. The mistake came about owing to the report placing him at a certain village, whilst there were several village-sites, some miles apart, all bearing the same name. No one knew at this time whether the enemy wanted to go north or south. A strong point was made in the orders to these columns that on no account was he to be allowed to get away to the north. When he did get away, from the point at which the attempt to surround him was made, he slipped between two of the columns—one of which was held up owing to very bad ground being encountered—and, when clear, turned to the south. As he could equally well have turned to the north this move made it pretty certain that he was not yet prepared to return to German East Africa.

It was now decided to open a base at Mozambique; the plan of campaign being to form lines west across the country from Port Amelia and Mozambique, and, by so doing, attempt to confine him to the area between these lines. The East African Force based on the ports was responsible for the eastern half of the lines, and the Nyasaland Force for the western half.

The idea was not really a sound one. It should have been obvious to anyone that a few thousand men could not guard a line three hundred and fifty miles long. For it could only be by the greatest piece of good luck that a force sufficiently strong to stop the enemy would be at the point he chose for crossing the line. He had no line of communication; there was plenty of food about; he could go where he liked, and the bush was very thick. In fact, for days at a time, he disappeared in the bush, and all touch was lost.

The situation became exactly like feeling about for a needle in a bundle of hay. You only found it by pricking your finger, and when it dropped off your finger it was lost again.

So the enemy continued his way south, and crossed the Mozambique line; occasionally mopping up Portuguese posts, occasionally bumping up against some of our troops, but never being caught by a force large enough to hold him, or do him any real harm. As he continued south it became evident that Quelimane, and the settled area along the coast, must be his objective. The Portuguese again became much alarmed.

We sent men to Quelimane; an awkward port to have to use as no ship drawing over fourteen feet could get over the bar, also the way inland from it was complicated. Rail, river and road alternated as means of communication. Our detachment went up to rail-head to support the Portuguese there, and took up an entrenched position. Their detachment was attacked by the enemy, and driven out of their position, leaving some field-guns in the enemy's hands. Several attacks by the enemy on our entrenchment were repulsed.

Later the Portuguese, who had been driven out of their own entrenchment, joined our detachment. The enemy then made another attack, supported by the fire of the captured guns. The Portuguese crowded over our men, a bit of a panic ensued, the entrenchment was carried by the enemy, the men driven to the bank of a deep river and a good many, including the officer commanding our men, were either drowned, or shot, in crossing.

The way was now open to Quelimane, but the enemy, possibly deterred by the fact that they would be likely to find Quelimane defended by the Navy, instead of advancing against it turned away north-east. Great efforts were made by various columns to intercept him; some columns marching very long distances on very little food.

Travelling north, with one of our columns following, the enemy came on a company of King's African Rifles entrenched at a place called Namirrue. An attack was made and the place invested. The King's African Rifles held out well, but, after some days, were obliged to leave the place more for the want of water than from the efforts of the enemy. Meanwhile a column of King's African Rifles moved down from the north to the assistance of Namirrue.

This column consisted of, nominally, two battalions, but was very weak indeed—barely five hundred rifles all told. It advanced to attack the enemy round Namirrue, but met with disaster, one battalion being overwhelmed in the bush, and the other suffering very badly in covering the withdrawal of the remnants. The column that had been following the enemy did not get up in time. It had marched so far, and so fast, that it had got away from its supply columns, and, unfortunately, was in a part of the country where no food was to be had. It was also completely out of touch, its sole means of communication being by field wireless, which was of no use in the thick forest-country among the tall trees.

At this juncture—the end of July—there was very little opposition between the enemy and the Rovuma, if he chose to go straight there. The greater part of the force was either south, or southwest, of his position, or too far away to the west to get in his way if he went due north. Instead of doing this, however, he turned north-west, making for the rich food-country about Antonio Annis, so enabling our columns, by hard marching, to get in touch with him again.

Everything now pointed to an attempt on the enemy's part to return to German East Africa. Every movement he made was towards the north. Several times on the way he was attacked by our columns, but he always managed to make good his escape by the employment of his usual tactics of holding up the attack till dark, and then disappearing into the bush. Once he had a very narrow shave. If all columns on the spot had acted boldly and energetically he would, almost certainly, have been forced to surrender. Unfortunately one column

A GERMAN MACHINE-GUN IN THE BUSH.
(From a captured photograph.)

did not do so, and he was able to scrape past. This occasion was possibly the nearest opportunity we ever got of rounding him up. We were in sufficient force; we were on three sides of him, and had one of the columns only acted with the same energy as the other two, the way could have been blocked, and he would have had to fight it out against superior numbers of very good troops.

In any case the way for his march to the Rovuma was now open again, and he moved off north, followed, but not interfered with, by the column that ought to have stopped him.

There remained only one chance of getting at him again, and that was when he might have to stop to collect supplies and porters to carry him across the foodless belt between Lucinje and the border. We had a dump at Lucinje, put there for the supply of any column that might be acting in that area, and in just the circumstances that had now arisen. By some mischance this dump had been forgotten, there was no adequate guard over it and there were no troops north of Mozambique to send to guard it. If the enemy could get there before an adequate guard arrived he would have ample supplies to take him to the Rovuma. There was only one way of getting men there, and that was by sending them in motors as far as motors could go. So, by using every available motor, and chancing the supply situation in the south, it was accomplished just in time.

The enemy thought discretion the better part,

avoided coming into contact with our posts, continued on his way to the north, and, on the 21st September, crossed the Rovuma almost due south of Songea. East and west of the point at which he crossed were troops, Nyasaland troops to the west, and troops from Lindi on the east.

A few days later he was attacked by the Northern Rhodesia Police Battalion near Songea, and turned east to get away. We reinforced Mahenge and Iringa for fear he might go that way, and made preparations for meeting him south of Tabora if he turned north, as he was reported by deserters to intend doing. But, instead of doing so, he turned north-west, then west, passing south of Lake Tanganyika into Northern Rhodesia.

On the way he attacked Fife, without success, and was rather severely handled by a force of King's African Rifles who came up with him in the open, to find his men not nearly so formidable there as when fighting in the bush. When news of the armistice was received he was well into Northern Rhodesia.

Von Lettow was notified at once that an armistice had been agreed to in Europe.

A copy of the telegram received was sent, in which it was stated that the terms included the unconditional surrender of the German force in East Africa within a month. But when the full terms were received it was found that the actual wording of the clause referring to East Africa was quite different. It enacted that the German force was to be evacuated within the time mentioned.

Von Lettow had accepted the original terms, but when he was told the correct terms he immediately pointed out that there was a great difference between unconditional surrender and evacuation; that the former meant surrender of arms, and the personnel as prisoners-of-war, whilst the latter involved neither. When, however, it was pointed out to him that it was impossible to send his askaris to their homes with their arms he agreed to the surrender of arms of the askaris, and to terms by which the white members of his force were to temporarily give up their arms.

The askaris were very averse to compliance with this order, and there seemed to be a possibility that the surrender might not pass off peaceably. At this juncture Von Lettow brought his influence to bear, and matters were arranged by which the surrender was carried out without a hitch. Without the exercise of his influence by the German commander there might have been grave difficulties, for we had not sufficient men on the spot to enforce the surrender of arms by the askaris, had they declined to deliver them up.

After the surrender the German force was marched to the south end of Lake Tanganyika, and conveyed to Kigoma in Belgian ships. From there they were sent to Tabora and the askaris dismissed to their homes. Unfortunately a good many, both white and black, died from influenza, which was very bad all over East Africa at that time.

Von Lettow and the ex-Governor, Von Schnee, with some of the staff, arrived in Dar-es-Salaam with the first batch of Europeans, who were brought there for embarkation to Germany.

Everyone was anxious to see the man who had shown himself such a wonderfully able commander; whose determination had kept things going when all about him were ready to end matters by surrender. In person he was a tall, spare, square-shouldered man, with close cropped grey hair, and a clear eye which looked you straight in the face. He had the bearing of a Prussian guardsman, but none of the bluster and swagger usually attributed to such. His manner was just what it should have been, courteous and polite. He talked extremely good English.

There can be little doubt that Von Lettow, personally, came out of the campaign with clean hands. There is no reason to believe that he connived at any practices not in accordance with the rules of war. That there were many regrettable lapses from his standard by members of the enemy forces is undoubted, but evidence goes to show that he punished such lapses when they came to his notice. Several cases of ill-treatment of prisoners had been punished by his orders, and one of the first things he inquired about on arrival in Dar-es-Salaam was the fate of the men he had heard we had tried for such offences. When told he expressed his acquiescence in the justice of their punishments.

PORTUGUESE EAST AFRICA 129

The only thing that can be said against him in this connection is that, knowing as he did that the prisoners were not being treated properly, he did not take proper precautions to prevent recurrence. His difficulty was that he had not sufficient reliable men of the right class to put in charge of prisoners who were not, as a rule, anywhere in the neighbourhood of the fighting force under him.

Von Schnee gave a very different impression. He had not the open look, nor had he the manner, of Von Lettow. He struck one as being a small-minded man; not a man to be trusted; quite the sort of man who would not only connive at, but would institute, treatment of civilian prisoners so designed as to degrade them in the eyes of the natives. The difference between the two men was very striking: Von Lettow gave the impression of being a regular soldier, a man of outstanding ability and a gentleman; Von Schnee of being a man of the less presentable lawyer class, full of cunning, by no means a fool, but not a gentleman.

The work of the East African Force was now at an end. There was nothing more for it to do but demobilise; a fairly simple task, dependent only on the provision of shipping for men who had to be sent to all parts of the world. Arrangements for garrisoning the recently conquered territory had already been made.

On the 13th of January, 1919, General Van Deventer left for South Africa, the administrative staff remaining intact for a month to start demobilisation, and clear up current work. At the end of the month the force definitely ceased to exist, the command of all troops in East Africa now coming under the officer commanding the King's African Rifles.

It was with real regret that everyone said good-bye to the last Commander-in-Chief. In many ways he had taken over a very difficult task, especially from the personal point of view. As an officer of the South African Defence Force he took over the command of a force that was essentially Imperial. The staff were all Imperial officers, the troops were almost entirely Imperial troops, and not largely South African as they had been when General Smuts took over. He succeeded an Imperial General whom everyone liked, and whom everyone thought had been badly treated. He was unaccustomed to talking English, and shy about trying to do so.

In spite of every drawback he undoubtedly made good, and left respected, trusted and liked by all, especially so by those who knew him best. He was a big man morally as well as physically. Extraordinarily clear-headed, he always saw the point of an argument at once, and could, and did, look at all sides of every question. He had a very high standard by which he judged the conduct of all men.

His plans were always logical, always based on his idea of what he would do if in the position of the enemy commander. That he did not succeed in bringing about the destruction or surrender of the enemy force was not his fault. The plans were good enough; what really beat him was the country, its extent and its impenetrability. In the kind of warfare he was called on to carry out success must always depend to a certain extent on luck, and just that bit of luck was denied him.

On several occasions the enemy was very near destruction. The plans had worked out all right, but something interfered. In some cases it was the failure of some officer in command of a body of troops, in others of the troops themselves, in others again it was the country that was against success. He was a great optimist, and never disheartened by the failure to bring the enemy to book. No doubt he occasionally took risks, but before doing so he always went thoroughly into the question at issue, and only took such when he thought the situation warranted it, at the same time thoroughly realising the risk he was taking.

Of course, some people who had decisions given against them were dissatisfied. On many subjects he had fixed ideas which could not be shaken, but however dissatisfied individuals may have been they knew that their cases, whatever they were, had been thoroughly gone into. That in some cases he made mistakes is probable, but who does not make mistakes?

CHAPTER VIII

ADMINISTRATION

Difficulties—Changing conditions: as to troops, area, labour, etc.—Shipping—Opening up new ports—Work the ships had to do—Dar-es-Salaam as main base and clearing-house—Petrol and petrol ships—Difficulties and danger of transport of petrol—Forecast of operations, even for short periods ahead, added to difficulties—Purchase of food in Portuguese East Africa—Composition of administrative staff—General Smuts, Commander of forces in field rather than in control of whole force, including administration—Personality of officers chiefly concerned with administration, and how it affected the force—Regulations and their reading—Conditions of East Africa not those contemplated by compiler of regulations—Task of I.G.C. very onerous—General success of supply.

ADMINISTRATION in East Africa had two sorts of difficulties to contend with, those natural and those artificial. By natural difficulties are meant those due to the composition of the force, to the distance from sources of supply, to the shipping shortage, to the country and climate. By artificial difficulties, those due to want of suitable organisation, the idiosyncrasies of chief administrative officers, and deliberate obstruction on the part of some who had to do with the supply of the force.

The conditions under which administration was carried on were for ever changing; not only by the extension of the line of communications, which, of

ADMINISTRATION

course, was to be expected, but in the character of the force and the supplies it required, the means of getting the supplies, and the means of getting them to the troops.

On the arrival of the East African Force in the country there was only one port in use, Killindini. At a later date there were eight ports in use. But at first, and when only the one port was in use, the troops were mostly near rail-head. Later there were more than a thousand miles of so-called road in use at one time, and the troops were more than two hundred miles away from the base ports on which they were dependent.

The change came about gradually. First one port and then another was opened as the operations extended southwards. For some months a particular port would be the important one; then another rose in importance, in its turn to become of little use, until the return to the north raised it again to the first place.

Transport was always short; generally there was not enough in the country; often an undue proportion of what there was could not be used owing to the ill-treatment it received in running over the bad roads. Animal transport was almost impossible because all animals were fly-struck within a few weeks, and died in another few weeks. Porter-transport had to be used largely, but the supply was not inexhaustible. It is an extravagant form of transport, and involved a great deal of suffering.

When the East African Force came into being

the troops composing it included East African local forces, Europeans on a special rate of pay—a very liberal rate compared with others. A Rhodesian regiment whose rate of pay was doubtful—it had been enlisted on a rate which was not specified, but was to be the same as that prevailing in the country in which it might be serving. It naturally claimed the rate given to the local forces, whilst the War Office contended that ordinary British rates were the real rates prevailing. South African troops, who were paid at English rates, with a special addition given by their own government. British and Indian regiments on their ordinary rates, and one battalion of King's African Rifles on a varying scale.

In the course of the campaign more South Africans came to the force; a Nigerian Brigade and a Gold Coast Regiment came and went; West Indian regiments did the same; men had to be enlisted in South Africa and India at special rates, often very high rates. In the late stages of the campaign, and of fighting troops, nothing but King's African Rifles remained. There were still departmental troops of all sorts; British, South African, Indian, Chinese, and of course East African.

The Native Labour Corps rose from what had been quite a manageable number in the early months of 1916 to something near a hundred and fifty thousand in 1917. Altogether well over a quarter of a million native labourers must have passed through the hands of the department. Besides the

ADMINISTRATION

men recruited in East Africa corps of labourers came from the west coast, and from the Seychelles. Cape boys came to look after animals. The Bishop of Zanzibar raised a corps in that island and came over in command of it.

Another great activity was the provision of slaughter cattle. Much of East Africa is unsuited to any animals except game, owing to the prevalence of fly. Cattle had to be bought in the districts where they could exist, and brought down to the railway by routes which did not traverse fly belts, so involving very long journeys. In addition, cattle were bought at the Cape, and in Rhodesia, and shipped in special animal ships to the ports at which supplies were required.

Shipping played a great part in the campaign. Shortage of ships, and accidents and delays, were the causes of some of the worst thrills to the administration during the latter part of the campaign.

When the conditions are looked at this is not to be wondered at. Eight ports were in use, and at not one of them could any ship be brought alongside a wharf. At most of the ports there were other limitations. Lindi could not be used by ships over four hundred feet long. Dar-es-Salaam was limited to ships of five hundred feet in length. Quelimane to ships of under fourteen feet draft. At Port Amelia the road inland started from the opposite side of the bay to that on which the town was situated, consequently no ships could approach the shore on that side; everything had to be unloaded on the town side, placed in lighters, and the lighters towed across the eight miles at high tide. At low tide they grounded on the mud some distance out, and the stores were unloaded and carried ashore. At Kilwa the landing place was some distance from the base and poisonously unhealthy. At Lindi the light railway started from some miles up a creek, and stores had to be taken up in lighters. All shipping and landing had to be carried out by tugs and lighters, and there were never too many of either.

Shipping had to be used economically, a very difficult condition in the circumstances. There were so many things for ships to do. Inward there were men and stores to be brought from the Cape and India. All stores and men from England were transhipped at the Cape; some of them twice, at Cape Town and again at Durban. Horses and cattle, fresh vegetables, various stores, as well as men for special work; and a small, very small, number of men, who had been sent down sick to the base hospitals in South Africa, had to be brought up. Special ships were told off for this latter work, and, on the whole, the service was fairly regular. Occasionally there were very annoying delays; ships were sent on to Cape Town to be docked when there were stores lying at Durban the force urgently needed.

It was the coastal work that was most difficult to arrange, and the arrangement of which caused most friction with the Naval Transport Department.

ADMINISTRATION

There were so many jobs to be done. From Killindini came regiments of King's African Rifles, as they were raised and became fit for service in the field; reinforcements for the regiments already with the force; porters in large numbers; locally purchased supplies; men returning from hospitals and convalescent homes.

Into Killindini went sick white men, sick King's African Rifles and sick porters. Supplies for the King's African Rifles in the way of ordnance equipment, medical stores and comforts; personnel sent out from England as officers and non-commissioned officers for the new King's African Rifles battalions.

Dar-es-Salaam was the clearing house of the force from the time it was occupied up to the close of military movements. Into Dar-es-Salaam came very nearly everything; the main exceptions were white personnel from England for the King's African Rifles, cattle for troops operating from southern ports, and fresh vegetables for the hospitals at the ports. In Dar-es-Salaam were the storehouses for the whole campaign, and the workshops for big work in reconditioning cars, and for doing all ordnance and engineer work. With the exceptions mentioned all the forces in the field were supplied with everything from this main storehouse. In consequence much coming and going of shipping occurred in Dar-es-Salaam harbour.

There was a good deal of ill-informed criticism as to the creation of Dar-es-Salaam as so very complete a store and clearing house. Looked at superficially it does seem wrong that anything intended for troops operating from, say, Port Amelia as a base should come from the Cape to Dar-es-Salaam, and then be sent to Port Amelia. But had it been possible to load a ship at Durban in such a way that she would have been able to discharge each part of her cargo wanted at the various ports on the way up all would have been well, but this was not possible. To carry out such a plan would have meant long delays of all ships on the way up from the Cape.

Among the wants of the ports there were always many things that could only be supplied from Dar-es-Salaam. Things manufactured in the workshops there; ordnance stores; medical stores; engineer stores; parts of consignments sent from England, which it would have been impossible to sort out at the Cape. So that, although some of the stores had to travel an extra distance, the scheme of making Dar-es-Salaam the central depot really economised shipping. Had it been possible to transfer the clearing-house to Durban, lock, stock, and barrel, matters might have been different, but such a transfer was not possible.

Owing to the time it took to get things from oversea sources of supply, and the uncertainty of a regular supply being kept up, it was decided that considerable reserves of all supplies must be kept in the country. Raiders might hold up supplies from India, as indeed happened. No ship came from there for nearly two months owing to the supposed presence of a raider in the Indian Ocean, and because no escort was available. Ships coming from England might be torpedoed. The stock it was decided to keep up was sufficient for ninety days' foodstuff. Of this stock large amounts came from India in ships which did not pass near the out ports, and so came direct to Dar-es-Salaam. The ships that brought it were not under control of the naval transport officer in East Africa, and therefore could not be used to take their cargoes down the coast.

The whole ninety days' reserve was not kept in Dar-es-Salaam. The various out ports were stocked up, but care had to be taken not to overstock them, as they were deserted at very short notice. It became impossible to tell from week to week what number of troops, if any, would be based on a particular port seven days hence. First Kilwa was the main base of the fighting force, with Lindi as quite a minor proposition. When the force moved south, overland, Lindi became the sole base at almost a moment's notice. Then Port Amelia had to be deserted at the shortest notice for Mozambique, and to come into importance again when the chase after Von Lettow moved north once more.

The stocks dropped at the ports, for the maintenance of the troops based on them, were sent up the line as opportunity offered; but when the line was suddenly left there remained supplies unevenly distributed over some two hundred miles of road. All the transport had moved away with the fighting troops; there was, in consequence, no way of getting these supplies back to the port, and so making them available again.

Those stocks actually at the port could be sent down to the new port by sea, with one exception, and that a vital one. Petrol could not be sent because there was no petrol ship on the coast. The N.T.O. would not allow petrol to be sent in an ordinary ship, and very rightly. One such ship was burnt, with a cargo of petrol aboard, in Killindini harbour, and another ship which had been used for carrying petrol was very seriously damaged by fire on her next voyage, probably owing to fumes which remained in her holds.

This inability to move petrol was a source of very great anxiety to the administration. Petrol ships bringing their cargoes from overseas were few and far between. When they came their cargoes were distributed between the ports as it seemed at the time they were most likely to be required; but the movements of troops were sudden, and, in one or two cases, disaster was only averted by extraordinary good luck.

When Mozambique suddenly became the base port of the main force there was very little petrol there, and no ship was due for some weeks. Appeals to the N.T.O. to make some arrangements for taking petrol from other ports, where it was available, were of no avail, and there was no suitable ship to make the transfer. Luck was with the force all the same, for the N.T.O. sent word that there was a petrol ship on its way to Beira with petrol for the Nyasaland force, and that, perhaps, some of that might be made available. General Northey was quite agreeable, provided the amount given should be regarded as a loan, and paid back before a certain date. This could be promised out of a consignment due to arrive long before the date named, and the situation was saved. Some time previous to this incident a ship, on its way from the Suez with petrol, was so long on the voyage that Lindi, at a time when it was the chief base of the fighting force, was down to its last case on her arrival.

One great cause of difficulty was the general staff's inability to obtain any sort of reliable forecast of future requirements. When Von Lettow moved off south from the Rovuma, into Portuguese territory, it was, apparently, at first intended only to take measures to prevent his return into German East Africa. This plan was changed. First the change took the form of protecting the coast-settlements in conjunction with the Portuguese; later it became a general hunt after him, with the idea of defeating him and bringing his activities to a close.

The original orders for the opening of Port Amelia and Mozambique were founded on the idea that only small forces were to be based on those ports. Even after it had been decided to operate with considerable forces from Port Amelia the general staff only asked for provision to be made for a maximum of twelve thousand mouths to be fed, at a distance of two hundred miles from the port. Eventually the actual number being fed, at that distance, was upwards of thirty-three thousand. Provision for feeding twelve thousand does not go far towards feeding the larger number.

The administrative staff, of course, got some warning, but the real fact that saved the situation was the possibility of getting food in the country. Mozambique was opened for, at most, one regiment to help the Portuguese. Warned by previous experience preparations were made for opening a full sized base. It was required all right! All the same, such uncertainty does not tend to make administration easy. The truth was that the general staff were a bit optimistic; they always thought they were bound to bring Von Lettow to book before there would be any necessity to make full use of the newly opened ports.

When it was found that food could be obtained in Portuguese territory the question arose as to the method of paying for it. The Portuguese could not produce any small silver to speak of. They said it was all in the possession of the Mozambique Company, who declined to part with it. The authorities said they would accept British small silver as legal tender for taxes and so on, but when it came to trying to get large quantities it was found that South Africa could only supply a very limited amount. The only thing to do was to try cloth.

So cloth was bought in the Zanzibar bazaar and used as money. Incidentally, the cloth merchants of Zanzibar, all Indians, thought they saw their way to make a large amount of money. Government must have cloth and would pay a price which would give a legitimate profit to the seller. The seller produced his invoices showing a price more than double the declared import value. The cloth had been passed through half a dozen hands at a profit, in each case according to the documents, which, on the face of them, were in order. Of course it was all a fake. The cloth was paid for at a price which gave a fair profit on the import price, and when these merchants saw their little scheme for making money was of no use they were quite satisfied.

Cloth did very well as currency for a time, but there soon came about a situation which might have been foreseen. The native ladies of the villages from which the supplies came had acquired sufficient clothes to last them a long time, and declined to take any more. Possibly they were afraid that the fashions might change before they had worn out what they had purchased; for there are fashions even in remote parts of Africa, and unless you have the pattern the ladies like they won't trade.

However, food was still wanted from these villages, and something had to be done. There was a lot of small German silver in the banks in Dar-es-Salaam, so this was sent down, and accepted by the natives. They probably melted it down and used it for making ornaments, or for trading away as bullion.

The composition and establishment of the headquarter staff were laid down by the War Office, and were specially designed to meet the circumstances of a case which were recognised as being to a certain extent abnormal. Generally speaking the establishment was that for an independent expeditionary force of a strength of, approximately, three divisions.

On his arrival to take command General Smuts found an established administrative staff, the strength and establishment of which had been settled by the War Office, and presumably suited to the conditions of the force he had come to command. He was satisfied to leave it at that. He went straight off to the front to take personal command of the operations, without troubling to go into details of the administrative arrangements. His only care was that his wants as commander in the field would be satisfied.

It may be taken as certain that a Commander-in-Chief of administrative experience, Sir Horace Smith-Dorrien for example, on deciding to cut himself off from his administrative headquarters as General Smuts did, would have satisfied himself that everything behind the lines was in a satisfactory position, and would have realised that there must be one responsible head with very wide powers. As it was the relative positions of the D.A. and Q.M.G. and the I.G.C. were not properly defined; there was much overlapping and, as a consequence, considerable creaking of the wheels of the administrative machine.

The personality of the two people chiefly concerned had something to do with this. The D.A. and Q.M.G., the head of the administrative staff, was a Colonel of the Indian Supply and Transport department, with the temporary rank of Brigadier-General. He was imbued with all the traditions of the service in which he had spent his life; very much inclined to enter into details; to centralise, in his own office, much work that should have been left to directors of services, more especially the work of that department to which he himself belonged, the S. & T.; but not excepting some things which should really have been in the hands of the I.G.C. The latter was a very charming man to meet, but too good-natured, too reluctant to give decisions which would be distasteful to anybody.

The Inspector-General of Communications had been selected on account of his knowledge of the country and its inhabitants. He was the Inspector-General of Police in British East Africa and Uganda, but had had no experience of higher military administration. He was full of energy, inclined to be hasty in his judgments, decidedly high strung, impatient of control, but, in his way, a very able man. Good man as he undoubtedly was many people found him very hard to get on with. He had the temporary rank of Brigadier-General, the same rank as that held by the D.A. and Q.M.G., and the directors of services.

Of course, it may be said that the duties of everyone are laid down in Field Service Regulations, and that no question as to the relative positions and duties of these two ought to have arisen. Regulations are made by men of knowledge and ability, men much more competent to make them than the great majority of those who have to be guided by them, though the latter are not inclined to allow it. The right way to read regulations is to recognise that in them are inculcated principles which must be followed in all cases, the letter of the regulations only being meant to be followed when the circumstances are exactly those contemplated by the wise men who made the regulations. A realisation of what those circumstances are is easy to come by from the regulations themselves. The letter of the regulations apply to normal situations; when the situation is in any way abnormal the seeker after knowledge must see how to apply the principles to his own case. Men accustomed to administration have no difficulty in recognising the principles underlying any particular paragraph, and applying them. Two men of entirely different temperaments, brought up in entirely different schools, may very well differ when it comes to deciding what principle it is that a given regulation—applicable to the letter to certain normal circumstances—inculcates when the circumstances are not those to which it was designed to apply.

The conditions under which administration had to

be carried on in East Africa were not normal, and particularly were they not normal in the relation of the I.G.C. to G.H.Q. administrative staff.

All provision was made by G.H.Q. The I.G.C. had to look to G.H.Q. for the implements of his trade; motor-cars, animals, porters, all his means of transport. The director of railways and the naval transport officer had come over with the Indian force, had always been in direct relation with G.H.Q., and were not specifically placed under the I.G.C. when he was established. They therefore continued to look to G.H.Q., especially when they did not see eye to eye with the I.G.C. as to his requirements. The I.G.C. considered that he should be independent of the D.A. and Q.M.G., and only directly responsible to the Commander-in-Chief. The D.A. and Q.M.G. did not agree. The I.G.C. said the regulations were in his favour in his contention. The D.A. and Q.M.G. pointed out that the regulations did not apply in this instance, as the conditions for which they were made were quite different. No definite ruling was ever given. There was trouble, and overlapping, right up to the time when the line of communications was done away with as a separate organisation, and merged in G.H.Q.

Very naturally all this kind of thing made the administration of the force very much more difficult for all concerned.

The task of the I.G.C. became more and more onerous as time went on. The staffs at the ports, on the lines running from the ports, at all posts, were under him. The administration of part of the conquered country was under him. The manning of all the posts, etc., was a very difficult matter to arrange.

There were so many qualities desirable in a post commandant, in an officer in charge of landing arrangements at a port, or in a political officer administering a district in occupied territory. Capacity for hard work, administrative ability, knowledge of the language, were all desirable. The I.G.C. had to be content if he got men with one of these three desirable qualifications. No one wanted to be relegated to the lines of communication. It meant a life of drudgery in a rotten climate, and very little chance of reward, however hard the work. The supply of suitable men never approached the number wanted, though numbers of men in the ranks, who seemed likely to be suitable, were given commissions for employment under the I.G.C. Some of these, indeed, proved that they were not at all suitable for any position of responsibility or trust.

The I.G.C. was, for many months, a sadly overworked man, constantly faced with possible breakdowns of some one or other of his lines, which would have meant disaster in that it would have spelt starvation for some part of the force.

On many occasions it seemed as if nothing could avert a serious break-down. Drastic curtailment of rations to be issued had to be ordered, down even to quarter rations. But, somehow, luck was with the

ADMINISTRATION

administration, and the danger was averted for that time; generally by enterprise on the part of someone on the spot.

Administration in East Africa was a very anxious business for everyone concerned with it. In the face of very great difficulties, natural and therefore unavoidable, artificial and therefore avoidable, supply was carried on extraordinarily successfully on the whole. There were times like that at Kondoa Irangi in the middle of 1916, at Iringa at the end of that year, on the Rufigi in the early months of 1917, and in Portuguese East Africa, when columns hard in pursuit of Von Lettow got right away from their supply columns, and men went hungry; but, generally speaking, a very fairly good supply was kept up. In the cases mentioned the shortage was the result of causes beyond the control of the administrative staff of the force, including, in that term, the I.G.C.

CHAPTER IX

MEDICAL ADMINISTRATION

Some of the problems—Early days—Developments—The base hospitals in South Africa—Effect of establishment of convalescent camps in British East Africa—Large percentage of sick—The carrier problem, and its solution—Hospitals in Dar-es-Salaam and elsewhere—Native African bibis, their use in hospitals—The Uganda native hospital corps—Mosquito brigades, and their work—Hospital ships—General remarks.

IN a campaign during which climate is one of the chief enemies the medical administration takes an even more prominent place than that which it must have in a campaign in normally healthy surroundings. In an unhealthy tropical climate like that of East Africa there is ever present with a force the menace of being rendered unfit for active work by a number of diseases due to climate, and which do not threaten troops in temperate countries. It is of no use expecting that any preventive measures can insure complete immunity from the diseases of the country, though much can be done. The work of the medical department in a preventive direction has many fields in which its activity can make itself felt.

The medical department in East Africa was faced

with many problems. The campaign had to be carried on over wide areas; the lines of communication were long and bad; transport of sick over the lines always difficult, sometimes impossible. At times the principle of evacuation of sick and wounded back from the fighting troops to a comfortable base hospital had to be abandoned for a considerable period, whilst difficulties of transport made it also impossible to get up to the front suitable hospitals for the treatment of the many sick who had to be left there.

In the earlier stages of the campaign, when all the troops were in British East Africa, medical organisation was fairly simple. The lines of communication were not very long, and the Uganda railway was convenient for the removal of sick to established hospitals. Good hospitals were established in Nairobi, at Mombasa, and on the railway at Voi, a hundred miles from Mombasa. Voi was also the junction from which the military railway branched in the direction of Taveta.

In and around Nairobi there were well-found convalescent homes, mostly started by private enterprise on the part of generous individuals, who gave their houses, and their services, to make the lot of the sick and wounded less hard. One well-known settler gave his house in Nairobi, and another in the country some thirty miles distant, as convalescent homes for the men of the 25th Royal Fusiliers, in which battalion he held a commission. His wife devoted herself to the care of the men who were sent to these homes. The widow of a distinguished General managed a home for other European soldiers in a house lent by two young settlers. The Maharaja of Gwalior provided the wherewithal for the establishment and maintenance of a home for sick Indian soldiers, and another, near by, for officers. An hotel, which had been before the war in possession of Germans, was taken over as a home for both officers and men. This home was situated high up in the hills above the great rift valley.

Up to the time when the force was increased in size by the advent of the South African contingent the accommodation thus provided was sufficient. The South Africans brought with them a base hospital of their own, which was established, in the first instance, in and around the Muthaiga club, about four miles out of Nairobi, and there it remained until headquarters was firmly established at Dar-es-Salaam, when it was moved there. Later, stationary and clearing hospitals arrived from England and the Mediterranean, and were installed at the advanced bases, and on the lines of communication, being moved about as the bases changed, and as circumstances required.

Previous to the creation of the East African Force there had been a species of dual control in medical administration in British East Africa and Uganda. The principal medical officer of the East African Protectorate was given a commission, and was in charge of the Protectorate troops in addition to his civil duties, the senior medical officer of

MEDICAL ADMINISTRATION

Indian Expeditionary Force B being in charge of the remainder. Many of the medical officers of the two Protectorates were given commissions, and did either whole or part time work for the force, in the hospitals and camps. To a certain extent this system continued up to the end. But when the East African Force was established the D.M.S. of that force took over supreme control. The senior medical officer of I.E.F.B. then became A.D.M.S. of the lines of communication, the P.M.Os. of the Protectorates continued to give their services in matters connected with the troops belonging to their respective governments.

One of the chief questions to be settled when the heads of departments landed in South Africa, on the way out, was that of the disposal of the force's sick. After some discussion it was decided that the base hospital of the force should be in South Africa, and that all cases requiring evacuation to the base, except Indian, should be sent there for disposal, sent back for duty, discharged or given sick leave in the case of South African units, and sent back or invalided to England if belonging to Imperial units.

On the face of it this arrangement looked very satisfactory, but, unfortunately, it did not prove so in practice. The medical authorities in South Africa acquired an exaggerated idea of the deadliness of the East African climate, the consequence being that very few men sent down, even of those sent down merely for change of air, ever came back. Some were kept a long time in hospitals and convalescent homes, and then sent to England, others were sent on to England without the climate of South Africa having been given a chance to make them fit for duty again. As for South Africans, it was almost a foregone conclusion that if sent down their unit had seen the last of them.

The question of invaliding was much complicated by this state of things. After a go of fever a man very often wanted a change out of the tropics to put him right again, and in a great many cases a change for a month or two made him once more quite fit for duty. There was no necessity for invaliding to England, or, if a South African, being discharged. When it became evident that the odds against a man returning if sent to South Africa for a change were very long indeed, it became needful to make other arrangements for giving the necessary change.

Eventually a large convalescent camp was established in a healthy place in British East Africa, to which men considered likely to get fit, after a short time, were sent. Change to such a place was not likely to have so good an effect as a change to South Africa, but the establishment of this convalescent camp proved, fairly conclusively, that we ought to have received back many more men than we had been getting. Roughly, about seventy per cent of the men who would have been sent to South Africa before the establishment of the home were sent to British East Africa, and, of these, about seventy per cent returned to duty. As the percentage of men sent to South Africa, who returned, was only, say, five per cent of the same class of case as those sent to British East Africa, the wastage in the force was reduced about fifty per cent by the establishment of this convalescent home.

The percentage of personnel constantly sick was very large, and the actual numbers to be treated and looked after were swelled by the enormous numbers of native carriers who had to be provided with medical attendance and hospital accommodation in addition to the troops of the force. In spite of the large percentage of sick the death rate, excepting among the carriers at certain times, was decidedly low. Most of the diseases from which men suffered were climatic; in many instances aggravated by hard work, short commons and exposure. The principle followed of getting the debilitated men away to a good climate as soon as possible led to recovery in the majority of cases.

For the treatment of the troops arrangements, from the first, were fairly adequate and complete. Where the sick and wounded did not get all the comfort and attention they should have had the cause was owing to the impossibility of movement during the rainy season.

The realisation of the immense organisation that would be necessary to deal with sick carriers came as a surprise. In the first place the number of carriers increased by leaps and bounds. Within a few months that which had been quite a modest organisation became an enormous one. But even then it was not at once realised what was required in the way of medical attendance. The carriers were natives of the country, and were, presumably, more or less immune from the tropical diseases which laid such a hold on European and other natives of non-tropical countries.

For the first few months after enrolment the men seemed to get on very well. The numbers had increased very rapidly, and simultaneously the work they had to do became more trying. Then, almost suddenly, it was realised that the number going sick was becoming alarming, and that the organisation for the treatment of this unit, increased though it had been in anticipation of a merely normal increase in the percentage of sick, would be quite unable to cope with the situation. The percentage of sick increased out of all proportion to the increase in numbers. Urgent requests for more doctors were met by the despatch of a large contingent from England; hospitals for carriers were established everywhere on the lines of communication, until there were more than fifteen thousand beds for carriers alone, and these were none too many.

In Dar-es-Salaam there were three large hospitals. The general hospital for Europeans was accommodated partly in the Kaiserhof hotel-building, partly in big office-buildings all round, in tents, and in the German hospital on the seashore. This latter held the surgical section, and the sick officers. In all the normal accommodation was for one thousand five hundred, but it could be, and at times had to be, extended to accommodate over two thousand.

The hospital for native troops was mainly a tent hospital, set on a low bluff above the inner harbour. The buildings of the German native hospital were also used, and here there was accommodation for about one thousand five hundred.

Another large hospital was the carrier hospital just outside the town. The buildings were originally bandas of brushwood, but, later on, a number of long huts with concrete floors and iron roofs had to be put up, as the bandas became infected with the spirillum tick. This hospital covered a large extent of ground, and accommodated up to two thousand patients.

Besides these hospitals there was a fairly big one for prisoners-of-war, and another for native of India details, not soldiers. As a rule all these hospitals were full.

At the ports at the base of the lines there were big stationary hospitals; those which had been sent out as such, or casualty clearing hospitals expanded as required. There were also hospitals along the central railway, at Mikesse—as long as the line from there was in operation—at Morogoro, and at Dodoma. The hospitals in British East Africa were kept open to the end; that at Mombasa chiefly as a rest hospital for patients on their way to Nairobi, at which place the hospital was latterly used for men of the Protectorate. There was a big King's

African Rifles hospital, and a big carrier hospital, at Nairobi also.

An interesting experiment was tried at the native troops hospital in Dar-es-Salaam. The matron there knew the East African native well, and talked the language. The idea therefore occurred to her of using native women as cooks, and for service in the wards. The women were very ready to come and work, and did excellent service. They were always clean and cheerful, went about the wards making men comfortable, cracking jokes, and taking round the food. At first some doubt was felt about sending in food by the hands of these women to the Indian officers, and they were not sent into the officers' ward. But all doubts were set at rest when the officers wanted to know what they had done that they should not be waited on by the bibis.

Later on this experiment was extended to the carrier hospital, and with equally satisfactory results, though the matron there, who also knew the native well, was, at first, very much against it. That same matron had an embarrassing experience during the influenza epidemic. A number of women came in with Von Lettow's men; many of them caught influenza and had to be taken into hospital. One who was dying gave birth to a child, and the matron, not knowing what to do with the new arrival, wrapped it in a blanket and took it to bed with her. How to feed it was the next problem. Feeding bottles are not articles of equipment for a military

MILITARY (SURGICAL) HOSPITAL, DAR-ES-SALAAM.
KAISERHOF HOTEL ANNEXE, USED AS A HOSPITAL.
MOTOR TRANSPORT CAMP, DAR-ES-SALAAM.

hospital. However, a message to the Red Cross commissioner, who supplied the hospital with articles not allowed by the equipment tables, found him equal even to this demand, and all was well. A day or two later the nuns at the local convent took the infant.

When the hospital accommodation for carriers had to be increased the demand for doctors was promptly met by the Home Authorities; the buildings were erected by the engineers; the hospital equipment was supplied from ordnance store; but the provision of a subordinate staff was a problem for which there seemed no solution. There were very few men available in the country, and neither England nor India could help to a sufficient extent. Then a brilliant idea occurred to someone to raise a corps from the mission boys in Uganda, train them, and send them down. The idea met with immediate favour in Uganda. The heir-apparent to the throne of Uganda not only helped by encouraging enlistment, but joined the corps himself as an officer, and came down with it to Dar-es-Salaam. The corps was very smart, very well turned out, and very proud of itself. It did most excellent work, and provided very efficient hospital orderlies. Its advent solved a very real difficulty.

Medical service with the force was very interesting to many of the doctors who came out from home, for very few of them had any knowledge of tropical diseases. In the hospitals, in addition to the more common tropical ailments, there were generally cases of diseases about which little is known by any but the few who have made the study of disease in tropical lands their work. Among others there were cases of both varieties of sleeping sickness, that variety of Portuguese East Africa and that associated with the west coast. Several cases of this disease occurred among Europeans. The first case recognised in the force was that of a European motor driver, who appeared to have contracted it on the road between Port Amelia and Medo.

In the matter of prevention of disease the most urgent need was the prevention of infection by the malaria-carrying mosquito. In Dar-es-Salaam war was declared against this poisonous insect. On our first arrival the mosquito was having it all her own way. Nearly everyone coming into the place went down with a go of fever within a fortnight. Mosquitoes were everywhere, and a good proportion were *anopheles*. At the head of the harbour is a large lagoon, separated from the harbour itself by a banked up dam along which a road runs. This lagoon is fed by a stream coming down a well marked valley through groves of cocoanut trees. In and around this lagoon, and the stream, were the mosquito breeding grounds.

Now, it so happened that among the officers who came round with the Nigerian Brigade was a man who had worked at the extermination of mosquitoes in the Panama Canal area. He was promptly put in charge of operations. There were some things which he could do at once; the cutting of the banks of the stream running into the lagoon, and those of the lagoon itself, so that they ran down perpendicularly to below the level of the water. This work was started immediately, for, by doing this, the larvæ then had no lurking places for escape from the fish introduced to feed on them. Then a brigade of small native boys was formed to go round and search for mosquitoes in the camps and buildings. They were taught where to look, and what to look for. Large scale maps were prepared, and every place in which an *anopheles* mosquito was found was marked on the map with a red flag, and steps taken to discover where she had come from. That place was drained, oiled, or otherwise treated, as circumstances directed. A separate map was prepared for each month, and it was astonishing to see in how many places mosquitoes were found during the first month, and in how few a couple of months later. The headquarters of the mosquito brigade was quite an interesting place. All round the room were cages containing different sorts of mosquitoes in various stages of development. On a shelf in the verandah were glass aquaria in which a variety of fish were kept. Some of these fish were delicate, elegant little things, and almost transparent, others ugly brutes, with big heads and rough skins, but all ate mosquito larvæ when they got the chance. Turn in a little water with larvæ in it and you saw the fish feed greedily. There was no question as to the good the mosquito brigade did, for, after they had been at work a few months, cases of malarial infection, traceable to Dar-es-Salaam, became few and far between.

Several hospital ships were working on the coast, others came from India, at intervals, to take away Indian invalids; others worked between Dar-es-Salaam and South Africa. For all ships Dar-es-Salaam was the clearing house, in the same manner as it was for supplies. The coastal ships brought invalids of all sorts from the base ports. In Dar-es-Salaam they were sorted out, some for South Africa, others for British East Africa, for the hospitals on the central railway, for India, and sent away in other ships direct to their destinations.

It might look as though it were waste of time and shipping to bring sick up from, say, Port Amelia, when their eventual destination was South Africa, but actually this was not so. The coastal ships visited the various ports at frequent intervals, clearing the local hospitals into the general hospitals at Dar-es-Salaam. There it was possible to sort out the cases, decide what to do with them, and keep them in comfort until the ship was ready to take them away. It was possible to arrange, too, that all ships were properly filled, and that the oversea ships were not unduly delayed.

Taking it altogether the medical department had plenty to do. The executive officers had to work full time looking after the patients of whom there were plenty to occupy them all. The administrative officers were for ever getting new problems to solve. Columns, of which there were many, constantly changing their composition and strength; constantly being started off in new directions, and all of them to be provided with ambulances. New lines of communication had to be staffed; rest places provided on the roads, and hospitals at the bases. The sick had to be brought back to the sea, shipped to Dar-es-Salaam, and sent off from there.

On the whole the work was well done. It would have been still better done had the medical department not been handicapped by the ever present difficulties of transport. The difficulties of transport included bad roads. The nature of the operations made it inevitable that sick and wounded should suffer badly at times. Conveyance for many miles over roads, or rather, should it be said, over apologies for roads, mere tracks cut through the bush; transfer from litter to ambulance, from ambulance to light railway, before reaching a fairly comfortable hospital in a base port, must have been hell for a badly wounded man, or one seriously ill from fever or dysentery. But it could not be helped. To get men back to a proper hospital, where they could be comfortable, and where they could be properly treated, was the best thing for them. Most men realised that this was so, and that the best possible was done for them in the circumstances.

From all accounts hospitals varied a good deal. A man may be a very excellent doctor, knowledgeable and capable in the treatment of sick, but at the same time a very poor administrator. Put such a man in charge of a hospital in an out-of-the-way part of the country and he is at sea. He has no idea of the best way by which to make his patients comfortable. He has had no experience of the shifts and contrivances of camp life. There may be many things at hand which he might make use of to give extra comfort, but he cannot see what they can be used for. Hence the difference in the comfort of hospitals. It was not the fault of the doctors that they did not know how to improve matters, it was their misfortune to be put in a position in which strange problems had to be solved; problems that had never presented themselves in a quiet country practice, or in a well ordered hospital in some big provincial town.

CHAPTER X

SUPPLY AND TRANSPORT

Getting supplies—Difficulties owing to transhipment in South Africa—Slaughter cattle—Fresh vegetables—Fresh milk—Distribution of supplies—Shortage of transport—Reason for shortage—Reconditioning of motor transport—Personnel, mechanics and drivers—Keeping balance of rations—Ordnance department—Variety and extent of demands—Some reasons for unexpectedly large demands—Mosquito nets—The Y.M.C.A., and the field-force canteens.

THE Supply and Transport department had a particularly important rôle in the campaign, as it has in all, and a particularly difficult one. Not only was it important and difficult, but thankless. The men at the front think little of the trouble and arrangement necessary to feed them many miles from a base, over apologies for roads, as long as they are getting their full rations, but they have a great deal to say when supply falls short of that which they consider their due. The Supply and Transport service gets little credit when things are going right, but any amount of blame and abuse should things go wrong.

Though supplies had to come almost entirely from overseas it was not the getting of them that troubled the directorate of the service so much as the distribution. Regular periodical supplies of foodstuffs were arranged for, and, with other requirements, were received with moderate regularity. The precaution taken to always aim at having ninety days supply in the country ensured there being sufficient reserve to make shipping delays a matter of minor consequence.

From South Africa regular consignments came at fairly short intervals, from India about once a month, from England at irregular intervals, and when shipping was available. Local resources were limited. Some supplies, such as mealie meal, beans, bacon and cheese, the two latter in small quantities, were obtained in British East Africa. The supply from England was made more irregular by the fact that everything was transhipped in South Africa, either at Cape Town or Durban, and sometimes at both. Direct ships were rare. The authorities in South Africa sent them on as the spirit moved them. When stocks of some sorts of goods, supplied from England, ran low, as they occasionally did, such as hospital comforts, and it was known that ample supplies had arrived in South Africa, it was annoying to find a ship had been filled with, say flour, of which there was no immediate need, whilst no hospital comforts had been sent, though telegrams had been dispatched asking for a good supply by the first ship.

This sort of thing happened so often that arrangements had to be made for a senior officer, belonging to the force, to be stationed at Durban, to look after the interests of the force, in this particular amongst others. The South African authorities did not welcome this appointment, and tried to put obstacles in the way of this officer sent down. These authorities seem to have had a great conceit of themselves, and to have resented anything in the way of suggestions for the better carrying on of the work, for they regarded such as unjustifiable criticism of their work. Heaven knows there was plenty of justification for criticism. In any case, and though denied a free hand, this officer managed to improve matters.

The supply of slaughter cattle was a great undertaking. Every possible source had to be tapped. Cattle ships brought beasts from Durban and Rhodesia. Large numbers were purchased both in British and German East Africa. Quite an elaborate organisation was required for this supply. The cattle had to be collected and got down to the railway without passing through a fly area. This precaution meant that they had to be brought down by round-about routes, sometimes involving treks of a hundred miles and over. The men who did the buying, and were responsible for the arrival of the cattle in good condition, were very successful, and the losses were extraordinarily small.

The supply of fresh vegetables was a big difficulty. The amount that could be raised in the country, though gardens were kept going, and the mission stations used for the purpose, was nothing like enough to supply the hospitals, much less the troops. Every ship coming up from Durban was supposed to bring a good consignment, but it was a ten days' trip, and if a ship was delayed, either in leaving Durban or en route, a large proportion became unfit for food by the time it got to Dar-es-Salaam. The Durban people had to order in advance, and to have a supply ready for the ship on the day she was put down to sail. But, somehow, ships had a way of not sailing on their proper days.

Another supply the hospitals cried out for was fresh milk, and to meet the demand to a limited extent a hundred cows were imported from South Africa, and a dairy established in a mission across the harbour at Dar-es-Salaam. The cows were stall-fed, and did remarkably well. They were mostly half-bred Frieslands, and, for many months, the average yield of milk was well over two gallons per cow. Of course, two hundred gallons of milk a day did not go far amongst all the sick in the place, but it did enable the hospitals to give fresh milk to special cases, and the doctors thought it well worth while.

The veterinary department looked after the dairy, and, according to their balance sheets, it was shown as actually an economic success. But that was a secondary matter provided the doctors were satisfied that it improved the state of the sick.

The distribution of supplies to the troops in the field was the work that gave the department most anxiety. As pointed out elsewhere there never was enough transport available. But the Supply and Transport directorate cannot be blamed. No one had, nor could have had, any idea as to what the wastage of transport would amount to. Early in 1916 it would have been possible to get plenty of transport. Demands were met without demur, but, at that time, there was no reason to suppose that the wastage would be anything equal to that which actually occurred. The unfortunate and unexpected necessity of keeping up supply to Kondoa Irangi during the rains, and then the almost immediate advance which followed our arrival on the central railway—before that railway could be used as a line of supply from a new base at Dar-es-Salaam—necessitated all supplies being brought right across from the Usambara railway by road. This used up so much transport that, thereafter, supply of transport was never able to catch up with the demand.

When attempts were made to outfit the force afresh with transport, in the early months of 1917, the reply was that motors were not available. Some were sent certainly, but not by the many hundreds that were wanted. No doubt General Smuts's announcement that the campaign was over accounted for the reluctance to increase supply. Under the circumstances there was nothing to be done but to try to recondition as many of the disabled cars as possible.

The director of the service established a big

repair shop in Dar-es-Salaam, and cars were brought in from the field in large numbers, reconditioned and sent out for another tour of duty. But a motor that has been broken down by running over so-called roads cannot be made anything like as good as a new one. Although, on paper, it would appear as a serviceable vehicle, actually its second life was likely to be much shorter than its first. The apparent lift of the motor transport with the force was really very different from the actual figure, and because it was usually impossible to use the heavy lorries on most of the roads. Such roads could only stand up against cars with pneumatic tyres.

Mechanics and motor-drivers were also hard to get. Numbers of both were sent out from England, some were obtained from South Africa, some came from China, and there were a few Indian and African natives available. Many of the men who came from England were only half trained, both as mechanics and drivers. One or two batches of the latter were largely composed of men of low health categories, who were very nearly useless in a country that very quickly finds out the weak spots in a man. Consequently they filled the hospitals, and a round of the wards almost invariably proved that any motor-driver in hospital had come out in one of those batches.

To try and supply deficiencies schools for drivers were established in Dar-es-Salaam and Nairobi, where men of various nationalities were trained; natives from East Africa and Uganda and from West Africa, India, and China. Some of them turned out quite useful, but a considerable proportion had not the nerve to drive over really bad roads.

In the earlier stages of the campaign much use was made of ox transport. There were large numbers of ox wagons in the country, but the supply of oxen ran dry, their life being very short owing to fly infection.

One great problem of distribution kept the balance of rations correct. The composition of the troops, to whom final distribution had to be made from an advanced post, was constantly changing. If the supply was from hand-to-mouth, as it frequently had to be, the rations might not be of the right class. Between the time of making up the convoy for stocking the post and the actual delivery to the troops the proportion of required European, Indian, and African rations might have changed owing to the fact that one column had moved on and another arrived. Again, it was never certain that all the cars of a convoy would get through. Possibly a car carrying some particular part of the ration—sugar or tea, or something else of which no great weight went to a ration—would break down, and, therefore, upset the balance badly; much to the annoyance of the men to whom the ration was to be issued.

The trials of the Ordnance Department were largely caused by the variety and dimensions of the demands made. No ordinary scale of replacements of kit and equipment will meet the wastage inevitable to a campaign in the bush, more especially when you have to deal with Boers and other South Africans. All calculations were upset, though the director anticipated demands being very much in excess of recognised scales.

The first shock came when the South African infantry left all their kits behind on proceeding to Kondoa, and then made urgent demands for complete replacement of all ordnance supplies. Another cause of excessive demands was that the mounted brigade, when a horse died—it lost so many horses that it had to be remounted twice in about five months—did not take the trouble to retrieve the saddlery. All they did was to cut enough leather from the flaps of the saddles to make new soles for their boots. They also, including some senior officers, cut up the khaki tents to make clothes.

The director was—and maybe he still is—convinced that when he dies the words " mosquito net " will be found plainly engraved on some internal organ. Urgent demands were common for many thousands of these to be supplied without delay. Sometimes because they had been left behind in kits, as by the South African infantry, or had been used as pull-throughs, and sometimes because the doctors had decided that the pattern in use was no good, and had evolved something new. All the native tailors in Nairobi were then put to work night and day to get them made.

Demands for hospital furniture and equipment were immense.

Pack saddlery for donkeys every one had different ideas about. The number of patterns the Ordnance Department had to make up must have run into dozens.

But this department suffered most from the length of time it took to get stores from England and India. Nearly all these requirements, whether material or made up goods, came from one or the other. Demands for new patterns were constant, and always very urgent.

Equipment for carriers was a very large item; jumpers, blankets and cooking pots had to be provided for more than a hundred thousand men at frequent intervals.

A very important service, that may take rank as a department, was the Y.M.C.A. In addition to its regular work it took all the management of the field-force canteens into its hands. In Dar-es-Salaam the men were better off than the officers. They had something in the nature of a club where they could meet their friends, play games and get light refreshments. The rooms were comfortable; there was an entertainment of some sort upon most nights of the week; the cinema, a concert or variety entertainment.

There was, too, a lot of musical talent, mostly in the ranks of the motor transport, and a really excellent troupe gave a lot of entertainment. On Thursday evenings there was a special show for officers and nurses, which was well attended. There was also a Carlile soldiers' club, which was looked after by the Church of England chaplains. This was combined with the garrison institute, which began in Nairobi in quite early days. There, too, were comfortable rooms where men could write their letters, see the papers, and get good meals at a very reasonable rate; they could also get hot baths. The number of teas served there, and at a branch in the motor drivers' camp, was astonishing.

CHAPTER XI

THE POLITICAL AND OTHER DEPARTMENTS

Duties, etc.—The Masai—Civil government of conquered territory—Veterinary department—Tropical diseases of animals—Field still open for discovery of preventives and remedies—Fly disease—Horse sickness—Inland water transport—Motor repair shops—The Chinese—Grave registration unit—Distances—Wild animals.

IN addition to the main administrative services, medical, supply and transport, and ordnance there were others which, though their heads did not perhaps rank as high as the ones mentioned, were nevertheless of first class importance for the smooth running of the whole. Some of them were subordinate to the Director of Supply and Transport, others were directly under General Headquarters or the lines of communication.

A necessary adjunct to a force advancing into an uncivilised enemy country is a staff of political officers to act as intermediaries between the invading force and the inhabitants, and to take over the administration of the country as it is occupied. In a civilised country it is usual for the civil functionaries to remain behind the invading army, and carry on the administration of the country under the orders of the Commander-in-Chief. In German East Africa the civil officers did not remain at their posts, so that the administration of the natives had to come directly under those political officers who had accompanied the force.

It is very necessary that such officers shall be men with knowledge of the sort of native that will have to be looked after, and possessed of some administrative experience. The political officers with the force were district officers of the British East African Protectorate service, and lent by the governor for the purpose, under a senior officer of the same service as Chief Political on the staff of the Commander-in-Chief.

The open country, from a short distance south of Nairobi to the west of Kilimanjaro, right away to Mpapua on the central railway, and from the Usambara railway on the east to Kondoa Irangi on the west, is the country of the Masai. This country stands partly in British and partly in German territory. The Masai are a strange people, and in time gone by they were the terror of north, and north-east Central Africa. They have since drifted south, and are now confined to the area mentioned; for the coming of the white man has put an end to their raids on peaceful neighbours.

Not so long ago supposing they coveted a bit of country they took it, killing, or driving away, the original owners. Though they have now been tamed to a certain degree they cannot be said to have been civilised. Their wealth is in cattle and donkeys. They neither cultivate nor do they work, but live on meat, the blood of animals, and milk. They have, at this date, become fairly amenable to light control by men they know and like. Those living on our side of the border had done good work early in the war by watching the frontier, and the man under whom they then worked was among those who came with the force as a political. It was important to be on good terms with the Masai, as we were sure to want to get cattle from them, and to use them for intelligence work.

As the force advanced political officers were placed in charge of each occupied district, but nothing in the way of any settled form of civil government was attempted. The officers administered the German law, as modified by proclamations under martial law, and it was a rather rough and ready administration. When the enemy had been driven south of the central railway, and we were in effective occupation of all the territory to the north of that line, and practically down to the Rufigi, the Commander-in-Chief thought the time had come for the establishment of a more settled government.

It is laid down by the Hague Convention that the government of an occupied territory must be a military government, established by the Commander-in-Chief of the invading army. The Home Government was, however, determined to bring this territory as directly under the Colonial Office as was possible. A senior officer of the Colonial Service was therefore appointed administrator of Conquered Territory. It was also necessary that he should receive his authority from the Commander-in-Chief. So, by proclamation, he was placed in civil charge of the districts north of the central railway, and as from the first of January, 1917.

It was thought, at the time, that these districts were well out of the area of military operations. But the administrator was in rather an anomalous position. Legally he was under the Commander-in-Chief, actually he was under the Colonial Office, and responsible to it for all he did in the districts handed over to him—within the limits of the proclamation. Beyond those limits he could not go, and any extension of these limits must be authorised by a further proclamation issued by the Commander-in-Chief.

Naturally there was considerable friction. A military government, directly under the Commander-in-Chief, would have been much more satisfactory, as well as interpreting the spirit of the Hague Convention. That the action of the Home Authorities was premature was soon apparent. The raiding party under Wintgens and Naumann broke back across the railway, and very nearly every district had to be brought back under the direct control of the Commander-in-Chief. The civil officers had to be granted military rank again (it had been taken away from them at the instance of the administrator) and had to come under the orders of the senior military officer acting against the raiders in these over-run districts.

By degrees the administrator assumed control of

DEPARTMENTS

nearly all the districts, until, at the Armistice, Lindi alone remained directly under the Commander-in-Chief.

For a time the districts not taken over by the Administrator were under the Inspector-General of Communications. Then a Chief Political Officer, in the person of Sir Theodore Morison, was appointed, directly under G.H.Q. And so the position remained until the number of districts left became so small that a C.P.O. was no longer required.

The taxes, on the German scale, were collected without much difficulty in most parts of the country.

A department that had very important work to do was the veterinary, under an assistant director. There were a great many animals with the force from first to last; horses, mules, donkeys, and cattle both draught and slaughter. The study of the tropical diseases of animals is quite as interesting as that of humans, and in both cases there is still a great deal to be learned. There is much that is common to both. In both fields of study the mosquito, the tick, and the tsetse fly are involved. The mosquito carries the germ of malaria to human beings, and it is more than suspected that the mosquito carries the germ of horse-sickness to equines. The tick infects humans with spirillum fever and cattle with east coast fever. The tsetse fly carries sleeping sickness to humans, also relapsing fever, and fly disease to animals. In the case of malaria the germ is now well known, also the species of mosquito that carries it. The germ of horse-sickness has not yet been found. It is known that it is a germ disease, but the organism that causes it is so minute that it is able to pass through a Berkfeldt filter, and is therefore too small to be seen under a microscope. But there is little doubt that the carrier is a mosquito; so protect a horse against mosquitoes and he does not contract horse-sickness. The spirillum tick is well known; it is found in old native dwellings, and all along the old slave routes. It is a most pernicious kind of tick, for it transmits the germ, and the power to infect through its eggs to succeeding generations. The east coast tick is a different insect, but it is well known, and by proper precautions animals can be protected from it.

During the last few years there has been a great access of knowledge in respect of animal diseases in Africa, and largely due to the investigations carried on at the veterinary laboratory near Nairobi. It was the general idea that the different varieties of tsetse fly carried different diseases. There are actually five or six varieties of fly, and it was said that two carried sleeping sickness and the others the fly-disease of animals. The officer in charge of the laboratory said he had reason to think that this idea was wrong, and that all varieties of tsetse can carry any sort of infection. He also said that the conclusion he had come to was that the different kinds of trypanosom, the parasite which causes these diseases, inhabits different areas, and that all flies in an area can, and do, carry the trypanosom of the area. The idea that this was not so was due to the fact that the fly usually met with in sleeping sickness areas was of two particular varieties. He said, further, that he was convinced that there were more varieties of trypanosom than had been supposed, and that some were harmless to equines but fatal to cattle, and vice versâ. If this is the case the idea that wild game are the only hosts of the trypanosom is erroneous, for horses can be the hosts of trypanosoms fatal to cattle, and vice versâ.

Although horse-sickness is still very baffling in respect to the mode of its conveyance to an animal, the chances of finding a protective serum or vaccine seem better. It appears that there are about five different strains of horse-sickness, and the protection against one strain does not give protection against the others, or, at any rate, not against all of them. As the germ cannot be seen and recognised, under the microscope it is plain that there must be great difficulty in knowing what strains a particular protective may protect against.

Before any definite result can be obtained it will be necessary to use up a very large number of horses, many hundreds probably. No treatment seems of much use in either horse-sickness or fly disease when once an animal has been infected. The great thing seems to be to aim at prevention of infection. Perhaps, some day, some remedy may be found, or a reliable vaccine or serum discovered which will immunise them. The veterinary officers saw much of these diseases. The losses from them were appalling, but it was shown that where advice as to prevention of infection was followed mortality was much reduced.

A department that only came into being, as far as East Africa was concerned, rather late in the day was the Inland Water Transport. A detachment was sent out to work the transport in the Rufigi delta, but, by the time they arrived, that line of supply had been abandoned, and the only line of inland water transport remaining in use was that up the river from Lindi, and worked by the Naval Transport Service.

The Naval Transport did not like the Inland Water Transport at all, and wished to decline their assistance altogether as unnecessary. G.H.Q. did not agree; they were not nearly so satisfied with the way things were being done by the Naval Transport as the Naval Transport themselves appeared to be. The director of the new department was sure that he could make many improvements in all sorts of directions connected with shipping and port work, if he were given the chance. He was also more accustomed to the language of the seafarer than to that of official correspondence, so that, in regard to the way things were being done, his language on paper was forcible—in conversation it was lurid.

When at last the D.I.W.T. was able to get to work, and was given a chance to improve matters, he showed that his claims were just.

DEPARTMENTS

To deal with merchant shipping merchant seamen, or the employés of shipping firms, are required. The Naval Transport Service in East Africa was run by the Royal Indian Marine; very excellent men at their own job no doubt, but not in the handling of merchant shipping, though they may be in trooping, mostly from port to port, along the coasts of India. They may have known something about the former job by the end of the war, but not so much as the officers of the Inland Water Transport did by a very long way. If, instead of attempting to boycott the Inland Water Transport at starting, they had welcomed their assistance, and had taken advantage of their experience, a considerable amount of shipping delay would have been saved. It would have meant, too, the saving of much money.

A very important branch of the transport department was the motor repair-shop, where a great many men were employed. After comparatively short service on improvised roads, which were really mere tracks—often only clearings through the bush—motor vehicles of all sorts wanted very extensive repairs. The main shop was in Dar-es-Salaam, and into this came a constant stream of cars from the field, to be reconditioned and sent out again for another term of service. There were no new cars to be had, so that old cars, really not fit for repair, had to be patched up and used again.

There were a lot of English mechanics in the shop, a few natives of India and Africa, and a number of Chinese. These latter had been recruited by some firm in China who must have had some dishonest employés, for a number of men enlisted and sent over as mechanics had no pretensions to being what they were shown on their documents to be. Men described as expert mechanics turned out to be barbers, attendants at eating houses, itinerant vendors, etc.

The Northern Chinaman appears to have a strong dislike for the native of South China, and there were some of each sort. Their dislike of one another led to much trouble, for they brought up bars of iron, wrenches and other weapons from the shops, and started pitched battles in the camp. For a time the officer in charge managed to restore order when fights took place. He was a noted boxer, and would go in with his fists and knock out the ringleaders. At last things got beyond him, and the weaker party had to be removed to the jail for safety pending its reshipment.

The official interpreter also had a bad time, and he deserved it. When, on their arrival, the officer in charge made a little speech to the men, the interpreter put in, as an addition of his own, that anyone who wanted to see the officer was to pay five rupees to the interpreter. The men paid until they found out they were being done, when they declared they would have the blood of the interpreter, who promptly retired to a dug-out armed with a revolver, and could not be induced to come out. They were very good men at repeat-work. They would make a dozen of anything from a pattern, and one could not pick the original from the copies. The majority were not very good at original work.

A department that had a most difficult part to play was the grave registration unit. Men lost their lives in all sorts of out-of-the-way places; in thick bush; in country covered with elephant grass many feet high, and had to be buried, more or less, where they fell. Graves were spread over enormous areas, often in ones and twos, and, though notes were taken to fix the positions, and often some prominent tree or other object close to the grave was photographed to assist subsequent identification of the spot, it frequently took days of search to find the actual place. Where actions on a larger scale had taken place, and the dead had been buried together, walls and fences had been put up, but it was found that these had been knocked down by wild animals. Elephants and rhinoceros seemed to take a delight in destroying anything that had been erected in their accustomed haunts. But, in spite of all difficulties, the men engaged were very successful in their work, and wherever it was possible the dead were collected in central cemeteries, which will be a special care of the district officers.

CHAPTER XII

CLIMATE, BUSH, AND BLACK COTTON SOIL

Effect of climate on non-tropical peoples—Variation of climate in East Africa—Malaria—Mosquito nets, and their use—Necessity of periodical change out of the tropics—The advantages bush gives the defence—How Von Lettow made use of it—The effect of bush fighting on the nerves, and some reasons for it—The general prevalence of black cotton soil on all lines—The effect on transport.

APART from the German troops the East African Force had three great enemies to contend with, climate, bush and black cotton soil.

The climate had its baleful effect on all services alike; bush was the bane of the fighting troops; while black cotton soil was that of the administrative services. Between them they had much to do with the fact that the campaign was not brought to a satisfactory conclusion.

Probably it is not going too far to characterise the climate of some parts of tropical Africa as the worst in the world, and German East Africa includes within its boundaries tracts that are as bad as any to be found on the African continent. The low lying parts of the country, along the coast, in the river valleys, and in all the less elevated parts inland, are intensely malarial, and the fever resulting from malarial infection is of a very virulent type. In addition to malaria there is the fever due to infection by the spirillum tick, which, besides being very severe in itself, leaves dreadful disabilities behind it. As in all tropical climates dysentery claims a number of victims, especially among those who have become debilitated through hard work under a tropical sun, attacks of fever, and insufficient food. Smallpox and cerebro-spinal meningitis are endemic in some parts of East and Central Africa, becoming at times epidemic. In some areas sleeping-sickness is met with, though not very many cases were detected in the force.

Along the coast, and inland at low elevations, it is hot all the year round. On the coast the thermometer does not rise very high, but it does not drop very much. For most of the year, in Dar-es-Salaam for instance, no covering is required at night, even when sleeping practically in the open. Directly you get to higher elevations, to above four thousand feet, though the temperature by day may be much higher by the thermometer than at the coast, it is not so trying, for the air is dry, and the night temperature is much lower.

Very few members of the East African Force escaped fever at some time or other. Protection from infection by mosquitoes is very easy to talk about, but not so easy to ensure. Every man in the force had a mosquito net, and stringent orders were issued from time to time as to their invariable use. Men were warned that to expose themselves to the bites of mosquitoes meant the contraction of malarial fever.

The malarial mosquito is supposed only to be active between dusk and daylight, but she is a fairly early riser, and is active in getting about her nefarious job before it becomes necessary to light a lamp. In those latitudes it is dark before seven in the evening, and men cannot be expected to go to bed at half-past five, but, until they are in bed, the mosquito net is not giving protection. It is therefore just before bedtime that Mrs Mosquito has her chance, and however careful a man may be about using his net at night.

Men were warned against leaving any parts of their bodies exposed to the mosquito in the evening, at least any more than they could help, and were especially ordered not to wear shorts after six o'clock. But total protection is very difficult to attain. There can be no doubt that when men really tried to take care of themselves the percentage of cases of malaria was sensibly reduced. In some medical units, where the officers in command insisted on every possible precaution being taken, and the men understood and appreciated the value of these precautions, malarial infection was almost negligible.

All the various tropical disease experts, who gave specialist advice to the medical department of the force, had their own fixed ideas on the subject of the shape, size and material for mosquito nets to be used in the field. It is difficult to say how many times the nets in use had to be scrapped in deference to expert opinion, and new ones provided at great expense and trouble. It must be allowed that the original pattern, an Indian one, was not of much use as a protection against mosquitoes. It was, however, found useful, as already recorded, in some units for making pull-throughs for rifles. It erred on the side of economy, as many Indian patterns did, for it required very little material, and was quite cheap in consequence. It was unfortunate that its successor, constructed under the eye of an expert, should have met with decided condemnation from a greater expert, and so on!

It is not an easy matter to arrange for mosquito net protection on the march. A bivouac would frequently be made in places where sticks on which to fasten the nets could not be found. To altogether put an end to malarial infection in the field in a malarial country is not possible. There is too great a chance of men being infected before going to bed, on sentry duty at night, or on night marches, but it is quite certain that the percentage of infection can be greatly reduced by the proper use of a suitable net and ordinary precautions against leaving more of the body exposed than is absolutely necessary in the evening, and at night, if then called on for duty. There is, moreover, no doubt that these precautions can be taken, under active service conditions, to an extent that has a noticeable result.

The tropical sun has a deleterious effect, both morally and physically, upon the European, and, though to less marked extent, on the native of India, and quite apart from either having actually suffered from specific disease. It physically reduces his tone, and makes him less resistant to infection by malarial mosquito or other insect. After a time he loses stamina, cannot do the same amount of hard work he was capable of before coming to the tropics. He feels thoroughly done up by the evening, without having done anything extraordinary in the way of work during the day. Morally it affects his nerves and his temper. Men become irritable and nervous, and are unable to concentrate on their work. The brain becomes easily tired, and, in many cases, there is danger of complete nervous breakdown. This often happens in the case of men whom no one would regard as likely to be affected in this way.

There is only one effectual remedy and that is a change out of the tropics. Physically to a considerable extent, morally to a much less extent, a change from damp coastal, or low elevation, areas to a higher inland part of the country, within the tropics, or vice versâ, has some good effect, but the benefit derived cannot be compared to that from a change to a non-tropical climate.

Men, physical and mental wrecks from the effect of a long time on the coast, improved considerably by a stay in Nairobi, or some part of British East Africa at an elevation of over four thousand five hundred feet, and came back more or less fit to go on with their work; but men equally bad, or worse, came back from a stay of equal duration at Durban, or the Cape, fully recovered, and fit for work.

After a few years in the tropics a change to a non-tropical climate appears to be vital to the majority of men to enable them to recover their proper physical and mental tone. This fact seems to be recognised by most men resident in tropical Africa.

The length of time a man or woman of a white race can remain in the tropics without a change varies with the individual, and is, of course, affected by the kind of life led. Perhaps temperament has as much to say to it as anything. The highly strung, nervous individual very quickly loses efficiency under a tropical sun; the placid one goes on much longer; but all feel it in the end. The fact that residents in the healthy uplands suffer in the course of time makes one doubt the possibility of raising white children successfully in the tropics at all, though, at first sight, they seem not to feel the effects to the same extent as grown men and women. But it is too early yet to say how a second generation, bred in the highlands of British East Africa, will get on.

This tropical exhaustion of vitality had considerable effect on the campaign. For successful action in the bush, steady nerves, readiness of resource and resolution, are eminently necessary. On more than one occasion failures must be put down to absence of these characteristics, and there is little doubt that this absence can be traced to the effects of the climate, though there may have been little or no actual illness.

The wastage of the force from climatic causes was very great, but, excepting in the case of the native porters at certain times and in certain localities, the death-rate was surprisingly low. It is not, however, meant to suggest that it was not serious, but, considering the number of men who were constantly sick, it seemed that the number of deaths might have been expected to be higher. Prompt invaliding to a good climate had, in all probability, much effect in keeping down the death-rate.

A great part of the area of East Africa, British, German and Portuguese, is covered with bush; rough bush-covered hills, and valleys of high, elephant grass. To the defender a bush-covered country of this description gives an advantage it is hard to estimate.

Strategically the East African Force was always the attacker, tactically nearly always so. Thus, the bush was a distinct advantage to the enemy. He was anxious to avoid general actions, and it was the bush that enabled him to avoid them. Time and again our columns, when following him, especially during the later stages of the campaign, found themselves held up by machine-gun fire towards the end of a day's march. It was impossible to see anything, impossible to tell whether we were being opposed by a rear-guard, or were up against the whole enemy force. By the time the situation could be cleared up, the flanks of the enemy found and preparations made for an attack, it was dark. Nothing could then be done till morning, by which time the enemy had disappeared into the bush, and, quite possibly, touch lost for some days, when much the same thing happened again.

The enemy were adepts at posting rear-guards in hilly, bush-covered country, where they could see without being seen, and could, for this reason, hold up an attacking force for hours. Bush, therefore, went a long way towards neutralising the advantage the British force had in the matter of equipment.

In thick bush artillery is of very little use. Aeroplanes, as long as they were available, could see very little. But, in the later stages, there were no aeroplanes with the force. It was also almost impossible for columns to keep touch in the bush, and attempts at combined movements, by which alone was there any chance of rounding up the enemy, were generally unsuccessful from this cause. Columns could be quite near one another without knowing it.

Bush made the fog of war indeed impenetrable. A thick bush country is without useful landmarks; the country was very imperfectly surveyed; the positions of villages were doubtful; even the courses of rivers were not known with approximate accuracy; consequently the combined action of columns was extraordinarily difficult to encompass.

Fighting in thick bush is also extraordinarily trying to the nerves. It means advancing in the dark as far as sight goes, and never knowing when some concealed machine-gun will open fire. To men run down by hard work under a tropical sun and fever the strain is almost more than they can bear. The constant expectation of fire being opened does not prevent the actual opening being in the nature of a surprise. To the enemy on the defensive there is none of this, for he is ready, and watching for a movement in the bush.

Everyone who has done any big game shooting in bush or jungle knows how hard it is to spot an animal that stands quite still. The movement of an ear, the flick of a tail will betray an animal that would have been passed by had it not been for this movement. The defender, as long as he keeps still in the bush, is very unlikely to be seen. The advancing attacker is of necessity on the move, and so reveals himself. The defender in the bush has, thus, a greater advantage than in the open, the advantage of seeing without being seen, the advantage of inflicting surprise on the attacker. It was the advantage the bush gave the enemy that enabled him to carry on for so long, and but for that advantage there can be no doubt that the end would have come months before the Armistice put an end to the campaign.

Just as bush hampered the fighting man black cotton soil hampered the supply services. The land lines of communication from the many sea-bases were very long; by them the fighting forces had to be fed, and these were never free from the menace of a break-down owing to the presence on every one of them of streaks of black cotton soil. In dry weather this soil stands up fairly well to wheeled traffic; a moderate fall of rain makes it impassable for motors; a little more and no wheeled transport can be used; a heavy fall makes it impassable for any transport except porters, and it may attain a condition that renders it impassable even for them. What may to-day be a fair, hard road, over which motors can work with ease, may to-morrow be a sea of sticky, black mud into which men sink to the waist.

East Africa is streaked with this soil, some streaks only a few hundred yards wide, others many miles. The narrower streaks can be dealt with by corduroying, but with the wider streaks this is not possible. It was the presence of this soil that made the supply of Kondoa Irangi so difficult, and caused the destruction of the South African troops. It was the cause of the break-down of the line from Dodoma to Iringa, with the result that the porters there suffered untold hardships. It was the same cause that brought about the semi-starvation of the Nigerians across the Rufigi in the early days of 1917, and made the supply of the troops in the Kilwa area so precarious at the same time. It wore out all transport. It killed numbers of porters.

Though there are regular wet and dry seasons in East Africa, as there are in all tropical climates, the seasons are not as distinct there as they are in some parts. There is danger of rain at all times, the menace of a break-down is, therefore, never absent. In any month there may be a heavy fall of rain which will make the black cotton soil streaks impassable for many days. For this reason the impossibility of using wheeled transport in the rainy season made it impossible to keep up a full supply. Porters were not to be got in sufficient numbers, and, even if they had been, there is, even then, a limit to the number of porters that can be used on a line, as they, in most cases, have to be fed from the base.

It will be understood, then, that the climate demanded that men should be well fed, and well done in every respect, when in an unhealthy area. All areas were unhealthy during the rainy season, and it was just at that time that this pernicious black soil prevented full supplies being got up to them. The serious amount of sickness among the troops would have been much reduced if they had been done really well during the most unhealthy part of the year; that they were not so done must, therefore, be put down to the difficulties due to black cotton soil.

The failure to bring about the destruction, or surrender, of the enemy force was undoubtedly due to these three factors, climate, bush, and black cotton soil. So, whilst every credit must be given to the enemy for the cleverness and persistency with which he carried out the task he had set himself, it is impossible to get away from the fact that he had very powerful friends in these three.

CHAPTER XIII

NATIVE MILITARY SERVICE

Africans serving with the force—Capacities in which employed—The King's African Rifles—Scouts—Machine-gun carriers and stretcher bearers—Carriers and labourers—Human transport—The beginnings of the labour department—Development—Rations of carriers.

A FEATURE of the campaign was the extent to which natives of Africa were employed, as soldiers, scouts, carriers, and labourers generally. The men of the King's African Rifles were all natives of the country, recruited almost entirely from the various tribes of East and Central Africa. There were a few men from Abyssinia, the Nile provinces and Somaliland. The police battalions were of the same material. Starting with three battalions, each with reserves, about a thousand strong, the sanctioned establishment had risen, when the Armistice came, to about twenty battalions; the total strength, with depots, being in the neighbourhood of twenty-seven thousand men.

The need for raising more battalions was seen at the beginning of 1916, and from then onwards, and from time to time, extra battalions were sanctioned. There was an intention to use some of these in other theatres of war should the campaign in East Africa come to an end before the war was finished elsewhere. The final organisation was, therefore, worked out with this end in view, and what had been battalions became regiments with several battalions, the number varying according to the number of recruits of each class likely to be obtainable. Behind the fighting battalions were training battalions, and behind them again large depots; the strength being calculated on the number of fighting battalions dependent on them, and the probable rate of wastage on home service, and on service overseas. The fighting battalions were organised on the model of British battalions, and machine-gun companies were raised as separate units.

General Smuts was much impressed by the fighting efficiency of the German askari formations, and considered it to be due in some degree to the number of Europeans attached to each company, but there was considerable difference of opinion on this point amongst the officers of the King's African Rifles. Some thought that European non-commissioned officers would be a dangerous experiment, because, unless they were of the very best class, and it was doubtful whether such were available, they would be worse than useless.

Nothing would have a worse effect than putting inefficient non-commissioned officers over black troops, or men who did not show a really good example in action. The decision, however, was in favour of the European non-commissioned officers,

NATIVE MILITARY SERVICE 199

and large numbers came out from England, together with large numbers of officers. The position of European officers and non-commissioned officers with black troops is one of even greater responsibility than with white men. To be a success they must be really first class men. The native soldier is a very shrewd critic of those set over him. The prestige of the British officers, and the few non-commissioned officers, who had served with the King's African Rifles up to that time was very high indeed. The askari looked up to them almost as supermen, and had some right to do so, for no men have better upheld the prestige of the white man in Africa than the officers of the King's African Rifles.

It was useless to expect that the hundreds of officers and non-commissioned officers who were now being sent up could all come up to the same high standard as had been preserved in pre-war days. On the whole, and considering everything, they were a very good lot, though there were amongst them men who should not have been sent out. Men who had suffered from shell shock, whose nerves were all to pieces; such men could not possibly be expected to come well through the trying experience of bush fighting.

Before any of these men were fit to go into the field they had to be taught the language. An officer, or non-commissioned officer, is not much good in the bush, where platoon commanders are often obliged to act on their own initiative, unless he can understand reports brought to him by his company scouts.

In West Africa Coast-English, a jargon not too easily understood by the stranger certainly, but soon acquired, is the lingua franca. In East Africa the lingua franca is Swahili, a mixed language, which bears a somewhat similar relation to Arabic as that borne by Urdu (Hindustani) the lingua franca of Northern and other parts of India. Urdu is the language of the camps, Swahili is the language of trade. Just as Urdu is a mixture of Arabic, Persian and the indigenous languages of India, with occasional words taken from the languages of European races, so is Swahili, if you substitute indigenous languages of that part of Africa for indigenous languages of India.

The new battalions were formed on a nucleus transferred from the parent battalions. The old, pre-war battalions each belonged to their own protectorate, and now became the first battalions of the various regiments. The 2nd Regiment had to be raised, first battalion and all, on the remnant left over for transfer to the first battalion when the second was disbanded just before the war. New battalions were raised, independently of the old ones, for service on the northern frontier, and on the coast, including Zanzibar. The first new battalions were sent into the field, much under sanctioned strength, in August and September of 1916.

Two years later there were thirteen battalions

KING'S AFRICAN RIFLES AT DRILL.
A K.A.R. SIGNAL SECTION.

NATIVE MILITARY SERVICE

actually on service. Owing to excessive wastage, and the time it took to train recruits, the battalions in the field were never at anything like full strength. Some of the battalions did wonderfully well. The first battalion of the 3rd Regiment—the original 3rd East African Protectorate battalion—never had more than six hundred men with it at a time, served in the field from the beginning to the end of the campaign, and had one thousand eight hundred casualties in action. Nothing, perhaps, compared with those suffered by many battalions in the trench warfare in France and Flanders, but heavy when this class of fighting is considered.

At the inspection in Dar-es-Salaam after the Armistice there was at least one man with the battalion, just in from the field, with five wound stripes.

As the Armistice came before the campaign in East Africa was over these troops had no chance of showing what they could do in other kinds of fighting. It is perhaps idle to speculate on the point, but there is every reason to believe that, as far as actual fighting is concerned, they would be fit to fight alongside any troops in the world. Their endurance is very good, but the real doubt arises as to whether their health would stand service out of Africa. It is just possible they might not stand it well. There is also the chance they would become homesick, a fatal and very common disease with the African.

The end of the war meant the disbandment of the majority of these battalions. German East Africa (Tanganyika Territory) had to be provided with a garrison, but the inhabitants being generally peaceful very few troops were required for this purpose, and the other territories had returned to pre-war conditions.

The scouts were drawn from the same classes as the King's African Rifles; they were soldiers in all but name, and were employed under the Intelligence branch of the general staff. Very good service was done by these men under picked British officers, and mostly officers who had experience of the country and the native. They were a thorn in the side of the German command; often behind their lines destroying dumps, waylaying patrols and foraging parties, and gaining information.

Next in the scale came the machine-gun porters and stretcher bearers, and, though not actually soldiers, the nature of their duties frequently took them under fire. Very few fights of importance took place without some of these men being recommended rewards for gallantry. They were specially picked men, trained in special camps, and attached permanently to formations. They were looked upon as part of the unit to which they were attached. They were really quite well off, for they were well looked after, and received more pay than the ordinary carrier or labourer. In spite of the fact that a good many were killed and wounded it would probably be found, if the statistics were examined, that a

NATIVE MILITARY SERVICE

greater proportion lived to return as fit men to their villages than did those of the transport carriers.

By far the greater number of natives employed with the force were used as carriers and labourers. In tropical Africa, West, Central, and East, human carriers are the normal method of transport. In the past there have been very good reasons for this. Animals cannot live in many parts of this region (wild game of course excluded) for, after a very short time, they die of what is commonly spoken of as " fly." The bite of the tsetse fly, as has already been explained, infects them with a living organism in the blood called trypanosoms, which rapidly cause death.

Fly is not found everywhere, but heavy bush and river valleys are always suspect. One year a particular piece of bush-country may be infested with them, the next it may be free. Another reason lies in the prevalence of black cotton soil, which, in wet weather, makes large tracts of country impassable for any form of transport except human carriers. It may be impassable even for them. Take the two things together and the reason for human transport is plain. The effects of fly can be mitigated by cutting the bush a long way back from the roads. Black cotton soil can generally be got over by the expenditure of much time and labour in corduroying, but in most parts of Africa the volume of traffic is not sufficient to warrant the expense of doing either of these things. In settled districts it has been done to a considerable extent. In unsettled districts human transport has been found sufficient to meet the needs of the country; so no roads have been made, narrow paths being enough. It may now be expected that there will be great development, for the tsetse fly cannot infect a motor-car!

At the beginning of the war it was necessary to make arrangements for a supply of native labour for transport, road making, general camp work, etc. The government was not pleased at the prospect of having to make heavy demands on the native population for these purposes, legitimate as such a demand undoubtedly was.

An officer of the Protectorate service was placed in charge of native labour, and given military rank. It was his business to get the men through the district officers and pass them on to the various units and services. The men were sent to a central depot where they were registered, medically examined, vaccinated, and given identification discs. The director of native labour had rather a thankless task, for he had two masters. The governor held him responsible for the good treatment of the men, the officers commanding units, and those in charge of the various services to whom the men were handed over, flouted his authority, and objected to his interference.

As the force grew so did the number of natives employed, but the one thing that did not grow in proportion was the European staff. At the beginning of 1916 the directing staff was quite unable to cope with the work, and there were far too few

NATIVE MILITARY SERVICE

Europeans available to look after the men in the field. It was a simple matter to sanction an increased establishment, but by no means simple to find the men to fill it.

Service with the carriers, as the department was called colloquially, was not popular. It meant all the discomforts, and many of the risks, of active service in the bush, and very little chance of distinction or reward. The only inducement that could be offered was comparatively good pay. The great desiderata in men employed to look after the carriers were knowledge of the language and of native way, also patience. The native can be extraordinarily trying to the temper, and tempers are liable to be short in the tropics. No man who loses his temper and ill-treats natives gets the best out of them; therefore, in an organisation like the native labour department, such men were very decidedly undesirable.

It was always difficult to arrive at the number of natives actually serving with the force. Returns from formations in distant parts of the country were only received at long intervals; many of the returns received were inaccurate, and the headquarter office of the department could not guarantee the accuracy of their figures; an error of some thousands had, therefore, to be allowed for. Men left a job they did not like, and managed to get taken on in another without any information being given to the director.

Early in 1917 the number was between a hundred

and twenty-five thousand and a hundred and thirty-five thousand, but, from first to last, it is probable that at least double that number passed through the books of the department. As most of the men had two or three names, which they used indiscriminately, and also made a practice of changing their identification discs—sometimes a man would appropriate the disc of a dead man if he thought he would get more pay on that, than on his own, when the time came to settle up—the problem of final settlement was complicated. Finger-print registration helped, but it was not possible to make it universal.

Human transport is all very well when the number employed is small, when only employed for a short time, and when food is available in the district in which it is working. Large numbers involve an elaborate establishment to look after them, and medical attendance. For a short time the African native does not suffer much from eating food cooked by himself.

The male African taken raw from his village (not the professional carrier who accompanies shooting parties, or regularly works away from home and learns how to feed himself) knows nothing of cooking. In his village it is done by the women. Coming in tired and hungry he is not going to be bothered to wait until his ration of mealie meal is properly cooked, he eats it half raw. Mealie meal properly cooked is wholesome enough, half cooked it is just the reverse. For a few weeks a man does not suffer from eating half cooked meals, but if his absence from his family is prolonged he gets ill with bowel trouble, loses condition, gets low-spirited and homesick, perhaps decides to die, and does so without apparent, or sufficient, cause.

In a country where food is not available human transport is the devil. A carrier eats his load in twenty days, so that his radius of action is not very great. The way numbers mount up when a long line of communication has to be maintained with carrier transport, through a foodless country, is extraordinary. To keep up a supply of three pounds per man to a force ten stages from the base takes just about as many carriers as there are men in the force to be supplied: and stages cannot be long as the men have to go both ways in the day.

When a long line had to be kept going to supply the Belgians south of the Kagera the question was very acute, and the limit was just about reached. Someone suggested that there was no need to worry, for, if the carriers arrived without loads, having eaten them en route, the Belgian askaris could eat the carriers, because they all came from the cannibal tribes of the Congo. Of course they were not actually " practising " cannibals, but they had filed teeth, and the people of some parts of Uganda were afraid of them. The suggestion was not entertained!

All the ports had to be worked on, and all the roads. The military light railways had to be made, and kept up by native labour, besides barrack and camp work, and all unskilled work in the stores and work-shops. At one time there were seven ports, and more than a thousand miles of road, in use. Rapid loading and unloading of ships was most important, and, in consequence, full gangs had to be kept up at every port, though, at some of them, there might not be many ships calling.

The actual carriers, the men who had to carry the loads, had a bad time, and their work was hardest at the worst time of the year, namely during the rains, when no other form of transport could be used over many long stretches of road. At these times the sick and death rates were really alarming. Everything possible was done to make matters easy, but they remained hard. If, try as you may, you cannot land at an advanced base more than half rations for everyone ahead of that base, the unfortunate carriers, taking the food on to the men at the front, can only be given half rations, when, considering the hard work they are doing, and the bad conditions as to climate, they ought, by rights, to be getting extra food. This state of things undoubtedly contributed to the casualties amongst the carriers.

No trouble or expense was spared in providing the carriers with a suitable ration. Special mealie meal was obtained from South Africa, much more finely ground than the local meal, and consequently requiring less cooking, and so being less likely to disagree if not fully cooked. Meat was issued very often, and some substitute given when meat was not available. The result was good, though it did not put an end to excessive casualties during operations, especially operations during the rainy season. But it did improve the general health of the men in a very marked manner. Before the influenza epidemic of 1918 raised the sick and casualty list to a dreadful figure the death rate amongst the native labourers was down to a peace figure.

CHAPTER XIV

DRAMATIS PERSONÆ AND SOME HAPPENINGS

Well-known men—" Characters "—Big men—The I.G.C.—Posts — Kenny — Ships' captains — Pretorious — Drought—Johnny Walker—The doctor the South African men swear by—Matron, South African base hospital.

IN a small force like that in East Africa there were naturally a good many people well known to the majority, quite apart from the positions of great authority held by them. At first, before the arrival of a Commander-in-Chief, and whilst it was still Indian Expeditionary Force B, it was quite an intimate little force. Everybody knew everybody else; the whole force was in British East Africa, and, though there was plenty of work guarding the railway, carrying out minor operations, and preparing for the coming big campaign, everyone spent some of the time in Nairobi.

Later on, when Dar-es-Salaam became the headquarters of the force, the troops were distributed over a much larger area, but the majority of officers passed through on their way to one or other of the forces in the field, and a very large number of both officers and men spent some time there awaiting passage, in hospital, or for other reasons.

DRAMATIS PERSONÆ

The personnel of the force was very varied. Many of the men who held positions which brought them into direct contact with large numbers of their fellows, base commandants, landing officers and the like, were " characters."

First and foremost in this category may be placed the " King of Maktau," the commandant of the base through which ran the branch line into German East Africa. He will not be forgotten by the many on whom he laid a clutching hand—as they tried to sneak through to the front without coming within his power—to be put in charge of a draft, or to be kept to perform some distasteful duty when they wanted to get up to the front and join their units. Few escaped, whomever they were.

Nor will many forget the hand-grasp of the mighty Dutchman, lord of the embarkation staff at Killindini, without whose aid it was difficult to get anything on or off a ship; whilst, at his bidding, a sufficient quota of natives, quick to obey his every command, shouldered the luggage on or off the waiting tug. Many, too, will remember his commanding presence later, on the quay at Port Amelia, marshalling a fleet of dhows to be towed over to Bandari.

Another figure known to many will be the genial, but, at times, rather harassed, Indian Army Major, the staff officer of the base at Dar-es-Salaam, who later became Town Commandant there—the Mayor with corporation. Talking of corporations, the supply officer at G.H.Q., the ever active Loppy, was as well known as most; at any rate he could not be passed in the road without notice, and the way in which he hurled his immense bulk about the tennis courts was a sight never to be forgotten. He was a cheerful, genial fellow who seemed to know everyone.

Somehow there were a lot of big men physically who were very well known in the force, by reputation if not personally, and amongst them the two gigantic brothers, the one who claimed to have stood up to Jack Johnson for six rounds, and pointed to his broken nose and gold front teeth as evidence, and who was further notable as the man who, when the I.G.C. went to inspect a post of which he was staff officer, seized the opportunity, afforded by the temporary absence of that senior officer on hospital inspection, to drink the contents of the two bottles of whisky which the said I.G.C. had hoped would last him his tour. The other, a jiu-jitsu expert, who got into trouble in various ways, among others for spanking a particular obnoxious youth with a foreign name, who unfortunately happened to be the giant's senior officer.

Still keeping to the physically big men there was one, a particularly bright star in the official firmament, who was known to a very wide circle, and independently of an official position which naturally made him prominent. He was a man who seemed to have a knack of being known far and wide. Coming over from India with the force that attacked Tanga he remained with the force to the end, most of the time as Chief of the General Staff, but with a period in the middle in command of a brigade. He seemed to know everyone and everyone seemed to know him. It was always this notable that the lame dog asked for help over the stile, and certainly help was never refused if the lame dog, whoever he might be, was in any way worthy of it. Among his well-known traits was a passion for strenuous exercise, even in the hottest and dampest weather. Unless you were prepared to walk about eight miles at the pace of five miles an hour it was as well to avoid going for walks with him. He loved good music, was a champion raquet player, a very fine lawn tennis player, and affected a supreme indifference for the other sex, but, all the same, seemed quite able to appreciate its more charming members when thrown in contact with them.

Another star in the official firmament, not a big man physically, was the I.G.C. He was everywhere, and wherever he was he made his personality felt. Many misjudged him, did not realise what a harassed, over-worked man he was; seemed to think that he ought to be pleased to see them at any time, and listen to their, often trivial, complaints, no matter at what length they thought fit to retail them. On the somewhat rare occasions when he was able to throw off his troubles and let the real man appear, that real man showed himself a genial, hospitable soul. Unfortunately, he was unable to detach himself from his troubles often enough; he took them too much to heart; they made him miserable and depressed; but an amusing story, and a little cheerful optimism, often served to tear aside the veil of misery for a bit, and reveal the real man underneath.

A well-known character, and one of the jokes of the force, was the director of post offices. He was a civilian, of the Indian postal service, with honorary rank. A most apologetic person; he apologised for his very existence quite as much as he did for the shortcomings of his department in not delivering letters for the force to out-of-the-way parts, which non-delivery was seldom his fault. But, most of all, did he apologise for the fact that the War Office, for some obscure reason of its own, insisted on making him a brevet Lieutenant-Colonel. Nor did he know what his friends in India would think of his exalted rank.

Another celebrity at G.H.Q. was the office superintendent; a warrant officer of the Indian miscellaneous department, with honorary rank. His office, where he sat buried in circulars and undelivered correspondence of that description (for which no one had any use) was besieged by people wanting to know something. He, too, was a much harassed man at times, but managed to answer most of the inquirers, and was a godsend to many who looked on G.H.Q. as a dangerous place into which it was almost as much as their lives were worth to penetrate, and whose great object was to find out something without having to interview any of the little tin gods in the office.

As everyone had to travel about from port to port at times the officers of the ships working regularly on the coast became widely known, and some of them were characters. For geniality the captain of the *Barjora* was known far and wide. He was one of the few who seemed really sorry when the time came for him to leave the coast. It was rumoured that his good luck on the coast did not stick to him after departure; that first of all his ship went aground in the Persian Gulf—a part of the world he knew better than most—and, to follow that, the ship on which he took passage home was torpedoed.

The captain of the *Tuna* was a very different sort of man, and not particularly genial. His knowledge of the landmarks on the coast between Killindini and Lindi was extensive, and well it was so, for it was generally accepted that he was unable to navigate his ship excepting by such landmarks. One of the amusements of his passengers was to watch him, of an early morning, trying to find out where he was, and peering through his glasses with a very anxious look on his face to see if he could pick up some mark through the morning mist, and then to catch the look of relief when he spotted the well-known white building that gave him the line into Tanga, or some equally familiar mark outside some other port. He had one other white man, the mate, amongst his crew, a man well past his prime, with one useful eye and no useful ear. His native crew, men from the west coast of India, were, luckily, very competent men. His ship was a small one, but, by careful packing, eight hundred natives could be stowed on board. It was said that, once, an over-sanguine embarkation officer managed to get eight hundred and one on board, and that the extra man was squeezed overboard.

Another pair well known and well liked were the captain and chief engineer of the *Ingoma*, a ship on which many thousands of men travelled backwards and forwards between Durban and the various ports on the coast. The two were inseparable; they had been shipmates for many years, and it was of no use asking the captain to dinner unless you asked the chief as well, for he simply would not come. A fine pair of merchant seamen these; the chief, of course, a Scot, a giant of a man with a handsome, ruddy face, white hair, and a very keen sense of humour.

Two others, celebrities known to all by reputation if not personally, were Pretorious the Scout, and Drought of the Skin Corps. They were both East Africans in the sense that they had been in East Africa before the war; the former, farming and elephant shooting in German territory, was by descent a Boer; the latter farming in British East Africa, and an Englishman. Pretorious was a big thorn in the flesh of Von Lettow. No braver, more daring man ever walked. He was always engaged in some wild enterprise behind the enemy lines; burning their dumps; holding up their patrols; watching their movements, accompanied by a few natives, men of the Scout Corps, or men of the country whom he had armed.

It was generally considered that he would have short shrift if the enemy caught him. No one understood how he managed to do all he did without being caught, but he managed it until his health gave way. Just about the time of the Armistice he came back from South Africa on a trip and to collect some of his property. He was in Dar-es-Salaam when Von Lettow came in, and, one day, when driving past the house in which Von Lettow was living the German General happened to be crossing the road. He saw the ex-scout, who had given him so much trouble, waved his hand and remarked, "hulloa, there's Pretorious," a much more friendly greeting than he would have given a few months earlier. Pretorious was the man selected by the Cape Government to destroy the savage wild elephants in the Addo bush near Port Elisabeth, and he said he considered this job the most dangerous he had ever undertaken, though he was not without experience in dealing with elephants, for, he said, his score was well over three hundred.

Drought was a man of character, and his corps one of the strangest raised in any theatre of war. Wild inhabitants of the country east of Lake Victoria, they considered they had a grievance against the Germans for taking their cattle; they also desired to be even with them and to get their cattle back. The corps was raised by voluntary enrolment. The qualification was the possession of a rifle and bandolier, which were obtained by knocking a German askari on the head in the bush. When a man had obtained the rifle, etc., he joined up, accompanied by a brother, or other near relative, who followed him on all occasions, and had the reversion of the equipment should the original owner become incapacitated. They asked no pay, only to be allowed to get their own back. They desired no uniform; they were not in the habit of wearing clothes; the rifle and bandolier was sufficient uniform for them; hence the official designation of the corps. The Skin Corps had a most honourable record. On more than one occasion they completely foiled German raiding parties, practically destroying one strong party which attacked a post they were holding; and, when the Belgians came to grief in their attack on Naumann's party at Ikoma, it was the Skin Corps who covered their retirement. Drought was as a god to these wild savages; a man of great character, great shrewdness and great courage.

The railway was not left without a notability. "Dear old Johnny Walker," as the director of railways was called behind his back, was certainly a bit of a character, and known to many, as were the strong-smelling Burma cheroots he always smoked. He had a constant grievance against the supply services for always wanting him to carry more food, and reduce the lift of material for construction, but he always managed to produce an extra lift when a real pinch came. He was always declaring that this and that could not be done, that the administrative staff knew nothing of railway working, but he always did it in the end. On one occasion there was a bit of work to be done—a wharf or pier to be made—the C.R.E. said he could not do it because he had not the men; Johnny Walker said he couldn't because he had not got the material; the D.A. and Q.M.G. said he did not care a damn who did it, but it had got to be done, and they might settle between them which of them did it. They left the room and talked it over. In a few minutes they returned and said that they played bridge together, and they had decided that the loser of the first rubber that evening should do the work, and the winner would help him with what he wanted, material or labour as the case might be. Poor Johnny Walker came home to die only a few days after landing.

The name of one Imperial officer is a name to conjure with in South Africa. The name of the man who commanded the casualty clearing station that followed the South African brigades when they advanced to, and beyond, the central railway, and came to anchor at Dodoma. There are hundreds, possibly thousands, of the men of those brigades, who would do anything for that man. His hospital was the first place where they felt they were receiving real care and attention. Fever stricken, tired, half starved, in many cases wounded, they were the men who had endured the hardships of Kondoa Irangi, and were pretty well used up. He was a master of improvisation; his hospital at Dodoma consisted almost entirely of improvised buildings. Beds, bakeries, baths, laundry, everything. It was clean, comfortable and efficient in every way; made so at a time when the railway was not open from Dar-es-Salaam, when everything still had to be brought from the Usambara railway, and the transport was only just able to carry the barest necessities, in the way of food and equipment, over that very stretched-out line. Made, too, to accommodate a thousand patients, with a staff meant to look after about a quarter of that number. One of the things that struck the observer from outside was the strict discipline maintained.

The South African soldier in East Africa was not, in the ordinary way, conspicuous for an outward display of respect for senior officers, but here you might have thought you were in a hospital of pre-war days. All the show of respect was given so willingly, not a sign of reluctance, not a sign of hesitation. It was extraordinary evidence of the personality of the commanding officer that he could instil such a spirit into these men.

Another notable character in hospital circles was the matron of the South African base hospital, established first at Muthaiga, near Nairobi, and then at Dar-es-Salaam. All the thousands of officers and men who passed through that hospital have a kindly feeling for the cheery, motherly woman, who took such an interest in them all, exuding good nature and kindness from every pore of her somewhat ample person. She, her sisters and nurses, had a bad time in Dar-es-Salaam. Hard work in a damp, hot climate is bad enough for a man, it is many times worse for a woman; but they, one and all, worked hard, often when sick with fever, often shorthanded, yet ever cheerful, ever kind.

CHAPTER XV

THE CAMPAIGN AND THE COLONY

The campaign—Was it a success?—Von Lettow's luck—Loss of life—The men at the front—Work behind the lines—Dar-es-Salaam—The harbour—Missions—German women—The German colony still undiscovered—What of its future?

THE East African Force was brought into being, and the campaign undertaken, with the object of conquering German East Africa. In that it was successful. It was continued to bring about the destruction, or capture, of the remnant of the German forces under General Von Lettow. In that it was unsuccessful.

From the time this enemy remnant crossed the Rovuma the whole German colony was completely in our hands. There were no enemy forces anywhere within it, excepting for the short period when, just before the Armistice, Von Lettow and his following crossed the south-west corner, from near Songea to the southern end of Lake Tanganyika, on their way to Southern Rhodesia. And from thence who can say where they intended going? Von Lettow hinted at Angola.

Looked at as a whole can the campaign be said to have been a successful one? In that it attained its main, original idea it may. All the same it was a matter for profound disappointment to those responsible for carrying it on in its later stages—commander, staff and regimental officers and men—that the remnant escaped, only to come in after the signature of a general armistice. It cannot be denied that Von Lettow had achieved the end he had set himself to do. He had kept a large number of troops employed to the very end. He had made us spend very large sums of money. He had shown great skill, but he also had had great luck. He had escaped by the skin of his teeth on more than one occasion, when just a little bit of luck on our side would have broken up his force.

Our force deserved to have had that little bit of luck. The troops in the field had a very hard time. Under the most favourable circumstances campaigning in a tropical climate is, to put it mildly, unpleasant. In East Africa it was much more than that. Frequently the troops in the field were short of food; very seldom, indeed, were they able to get the little comforts which count for so much under such circumstances. Of luxuries they had none. For weeks at a time they received no mails. There was little chance of leave, none, of course, of leave home.

Not enough shipping; not enough motors; not enough carriers; bad roads. The stuff the men wanted was generally in the country, and even at the base ports, though not invariably for shipping was sometimes behindhand.

On paper there were plenty of motors in the

country, but bad roads broke up motors very quickly. At one time when that which was thought to be a sufficient margin for cars out of action had been allowed, namely one-third, it was suddenly found that two-thirds were at a standstill. Sometimes a storm of rain closed a road to motors altogether. If the transport difficulties could have been swept away most, if not all, the discomforts of the fighting-man, not inherent to tropical campaigning, would have been swept away also—and most of the anxieties of the headquarter staff.

Many officers and men spent years without being away from duty, unless sick in hospital, and very few escaped that condition.

Besides having luck, as he did, in escaping our columns, Von Lettow had extraordinary luck in getting in supplies from outside. Twice at least store-ships managed to land their cargoes of arms, ammunition, medicines, clothing and supplies of all sorts, on the coast, and in spite of the blockade the Navy was supposed to be maintaining.

Without these replenishments it is extremely doubtful whether even the resourcefulness of Von Lettow would have sufficed to enable the troops to carry on. Of course it is a long coast line to watch, and the naval ships on the coast were not numerous. If report speaks truly the cargo of one of the ships should never have been allowed to reach the troops, and in spite of the fact that the ship ran the blockade. This ship was seen—just as she began to land her stores—fired at, and apparently set on fire. In reality the fire seen was a fire lighted by the Germans themselves, on the deck of the ship, with the intention to deceive. It was a pity the Navy did not stand by to make certain that the ship was destroyed.

For a campaign of this description the loss of life was heavy. Of troops and followers over four thousand were killed or died of wounds. The deaths from disease reached a total of over five thousand five hundred amongst the troops, and very many times that number among the followers.

In money, too, it was an expensive campaign. At a time when shipping was short, and very valuable, everything—men, food, supplies of every sort—had to be brought from overseas. The wastage from invaliding was very great, for all had to be sent away in ships, and the men to replace the invalids had to come in ships. The total number of men for whom food had to be imported was very large, including as it did all the human carriers. The cost of shipping was therefore a very important item in the total expenditure.

The men who had to undergo all the hardships of campaigning in tropical bush very naturally considered that those living in Dar-es-Salaam had a very easy time of it. In a way they had right on their side, the men in Dar-es-Salaam had no hardships to suffer; they had decent places to live in; they had enough to eat; they got their letters with moderate regularity—once every four or five weeks. They were not, however, idling away their time as some in the field seemed to think they were.

Work was very continuous; hours were very long, and Dar-es-Salaam is not a health resort. Very few, indeed, managed to keep out of hospital altogether. To those in responsible positions it was a life of constant anxiety, as well as a life of continual hard work. From day to day there was no knowing what the next twenty-four hours would bring forth. They, at least, worked hard to make things light for those in the field. Their success was not as great as they could have wished, but it was only by constant hard work that matters were kept going as well as they were. The force, in many ways, lived from hand to mouth, and that hand had a long way to reach. It was always the same cry, the same difficulty—transport.

This chief town of the colony, Dar-es-Salaam, is not a pleasant place to live in as regards climate; it is uncomfortably warm all the year round, and most of the year it is decidedly hot and damp.

As a town it is well laid out; good broad roads are everywhere, even in the native quarter. Many of the roads are planted with trees on both sides; the main business street with a kind of acacia, which, at certain times of the year, bears a mass of flame-coloured flowers, and gives a very gorgeous effect. The broad road running along the harbour, in front of the offices, is planted with a double row, on each side, of a kind of pipal; a big-leaved shady tree.

The government offices are fine, double-storied stone buildings, with broad verandahs looking out over the harbour; in line with them, on the road skirting the harbour, are the churches, the officers' club, the jail, the post office, the Kaiserhof Hotel, and various big business premises. Behind the offices are the government bungalows where the German officials lived; all well built, and mostly in self-contained flats.

The Governor's palace is in an enclosure of several acres, containing some very fine trees. It looks out to the east over the open sea, beyond the harbour, and must have been quite a fine building before the Navy shelled it, and knocked the upper story down, so wrecking the lower story in the fall.

The Governor's wife, a native of Australia or New Zealand, was indignant at the destruction of her home, and General Wahle, in his diary, says that she was so angry that she said she would never have anything more to do with the English. She kept her word, for when taken prisoner by the Belgians on their occupation of Tabora, she was sent, at her own request, to Europe by way of the Congo, and thence to Germany, in exchange for some Belgian women then in German hands.

A few hundred yards farther along the shore, and away from the harbour, is the European hospital. This is a fine building, and placed as it is on rising ground it gets all the sea breezes. Behind, and inland, are the houses of the unofficial Europeans. The whole place is very flat—only just above sea-level—and covered with cocoanut palms, which are valuable, no doubt, but very monotonous.

The harbour is a good one, with a very narrow entrance facing north. The outer harbour is protected from big seas by a row of islands standing off the coast. On one of these is the lighthouse, and another was used as a quarantine station.

The Germans tried to block the narrow entrance by sinking a floating dock and a big ship in the fairway. They managed to get the floating dock on the east side of the channel and pretty much where they wanted it, but they were not so successful with the ship. The tide runs through this narrow entrance at a tremendous pace and the ship was caught and carried on to the bank on the west side of the channel, and sank in quite shallow water. She was very nearly high and dry at low-water spring tides, and parallel to the fairway, which was thus left sufficiently clear to allow the passage of a big ship.

The channel, from the lighthouse to the entrance to the harbour, is not very wide, and a very awkward corner had also to be negotiated. The Germans had a good many accidents there, but our pilot was very successful, and never ran a ship aground. One ship did run ashore at this corner, but it was in charge of its own captain, who was not very good at reading signals, and tried to come in when a hospital ship was on her way out. In trying to get out of the way he got well aground. Inside the harbour there is room for quite a large number of ships, and a deep water creek runs south-eastward for several miles out of the harbour proper. There also ships can be anchored if necessary.

Christian missions in German East Africa were very important organisations, apart from their religious missionary activities. They were used by the government of the colony as a part of their administration, as adjuncts to their regular district officers. There were both Lutheran and Catholic German missions, and the Universities mission, with headquarters in Zanzibar, had large establishments in the Lindi and other districts.

When war broke out the members of the latter were taken prisoners, and only released when Tabora was occupied in 1916. They were not well treated. Some of the ladies of the mission, who were trained sick nurses, were kept to assist in looking after the wounded, and, on the whole, these ladies were treated fairly well, but were suspected of trying to communicate with us, and were very closely watched in consequence.

A good many of the Catholic missionaries were Alsatians, who, when we arrived on the scene, considered that they should be treated as belonging to an allied nation, but they did not all behave in too friendly a manner. They were also tremendous autocrats in their settlements. Converts who did not attend Mass on a Sunday were soundly beaten, and all converts had to give a certain number of days' work on the settlement-lands without payment; nor were the young women allowed to marry excepting with the consent of the missionaries.

What we most objected to was that they discouraged the natives from working for us, and if they came and, in consequence, could not attend Mass, pressure was put on them by giving their wives a whipping. Some of these missionaries were so aggressive that they had to be deported, much to the annoyance of the Bishop of Bagamoyo, a very determined prelate. It was said that he had excommunicated the Admiral, who happened to be a Catholic, because, in shelling some trenches which the enemy had erected close to the cathedral, a shell had struck the building while service was in progress. He must have subsequently removed the ban, for he became quite friendly with the Admiral.

The mission gardens were very well cultivated and produced a lot of very good vegetables, the consequence being that we had contracts with their owners for the supply of these to the hospitals.

The male German population was serving with the troops in the fields, and very few men were left on farms or in the towns when we came into occupation, but the women remained. There were large numbers of women and children in Dar-es-Salaam, Tanga, Morogoro and Wilhelmstal and in the settlements near Kilimanjaro.

Early in 1917 the Home Government decided to repatriate all the German population, but the shortage of shipping, and especially the fact that it was necessary to use neutral ships for repatriation, made it impossible to carry out this decision. They were therefore still in the colony at the Armistice. They were a source of considerable embarrassment, especially at a place like Dar-es-Salaam, where there were always large numbers of troops. A lot of houses had to be used for the accommodation of officers and men, and this meant that the women and children were rather crowded up in the remainder. They were kept under strict control; the quarter in which they lived was strictly out of bounds to all troops, and they were themselves restricted in their movements. Some parts of the town were forbidden to them, and they all had to be in their houses when the curfew sounded at half-past six in the evening. They were allowed on the beach in the afternoon and evening to get there the benefit of the only cool breezes ever blowing in Dar-es-Salaam.

Their maintenance was also a difficulty. At first they had sufficient money to provide for themselves, but, after a few months, their resources came to an end, and we had to provide them with funds. This we did by a system of advances made through a town committee composed of some of the leading Germans civilians left behind. The head of the committee was represented by the manager of the state bank. Later, and after considerable correspondence had taken place, the German Government made itself responsible for the money so advanced.

This captured German colony is still, to a very large extent, undiscovered country, for comparatively little of its three or four hundred thousand square miles have been opened up. Along parts of the coast, in the Usambara, round Kilimanjaro, in places along the central railway, and near Kilwa and Lindi, there are settlements, but these can be likened almost to oases in an unknown desert.

The thousands of square miles of bush-covered country, much of it hill country, may contain mineral wealth to any amount. Gold has been found and worked near the south-east corner of Lake Victoria, and mica in the Morogoro and Bismarcksburg districts. Coal has been found in several places, and, up till now, not a hundredth part of the country has been even superficially prospected. But, from what has been found, there is every reason to believe that great mineral wealth lies hidden among its bush-covered hills.

Apart from mineral wealth parts of the country are suitable for settlement by European planters. The Germans have grown sisal and coffee with success, and there is much land that will grow cotton. Rubber has been planted near Tanga, and along the central railway. Near Morogoro there are miles of rubber plantations, but it was said that the wrong kind of rubber tree had been tried. The greater part of the country is too low lying to be as favourable for European settlement as the high lands of North Western British East Africa, but there is yet much country not too bad for Europeans to make homes in.

The question as to whether it is possible for white races to settle, and bring up their families successfully, in tropical Africa is one that it will take time to answer. The result cannot be determined by the experience of one generation. Opinion in British East Africa, as already mentioned, is divided on this question. Some declare that there is no doubt that in the highlands children will thrive, and that the climate is just as good as any to be found out of the tropics. But some at least of those expressing this opinion have land for sale! Others say that the tropical sun has such an effect on the nerves of white people that a settled white population is out of the question. Certainly children born of white parents—natives themselves of temperate climes—seem to do very well, but there is nothing to go upon by which to judge the possible condition of the second generation. Time alone can, therefore, answer this vital question.

INDEX

ABYSSINIANS, 23, 197
Angola, 222
Antonio Annis, 124
Arab Rifles, 26
Aruscha, 63, 64, 65, 66, 96

BAGAMOYO, 73
Bagamoyo, Bishop of, 230
Bandari, 118, 211
Barjora, Captain of the, 215
Beira, 141
Belgian Congo, 16
Bismarcksburg, 232
Botha, General, 37, 50, 57, 59
British East Africa. *See* Kenia Colony
Bukoba, 31

CAPE CORPS, 96
Cape Town, 51, 136, 138, 166, 190
Carlile Soldiers' Club, 174
Collyer, Colonel, 58
Crowe, 41
Cunninghame, 45

DAR-ES-SALAAM, 67, 73, 74, 76, 77, 80, 84, 90, 92, 97, 128, 135, 137, 138, 139, 144, 152, 156, 159, 160, 162, 163, 168, 169, 170, 173, 183, 210, 211, 217, 220, 221, 225, 226, 230, 231

Dealy, 41
Dodoma, 72, 81, 90, 91, 157, 195, 219
Drought of the Skin Corps, 216, 217, 218
Durban, 50, 52, 136, 138, 166, 167, 168, 190, 216

EAST AFRICAN FORCE, 39
Edwards, Lieutenant-Colonel, 41
Ewart, Brigadier-General, 40

FIFE, 126
Frontiersmen. *See* Royal Fusiliers, 25th

GERMAN EAST AFRICA, 16, 23, 30, 33, 36, 37, 43, 44, 45, 49, 79, 84, 88, 98, 99, 104, 112, 113, 114, 115, 121, 124, 141, 167, 175, 186, 192, 222, 229
German South-West Africa, 37, 47
Gold Coast Regiment, 113, 117, 134
Graham, Colonel, 65
Great Rift Valley, 18, 20, 22
Guest, Captain, 39, 40
Gwalior, Maharaja of, 152

HANDENI, 66, 71, 97
Hazelton, 40

INDEX

Himo, 69
Hoskins, General, 57, 58, 83, 87, 88, 99, 100
Hunter, Colonel, 41

IKOMA, 95, 218
Indian Expeditionary Force B, 53, 54, 60, 153, 210
Ingoma, Captain and Chief Engineer of the, 216
Iringa, 81, 89, 90, 91, 102, 107, 149, 195
Italian Somaliland, 16

JASSIN, 31
"Johnny Walker," 218, 219
Juba River, 16

KAGERA RIVER, 61, 78, 84, 207
Kahé, 65, 66
Kampala, 18
Kenia Colony (British East Africa), 16, 17, 18, 19, 23, 31, 33, 36, 41, 42, 60, 61, 84, 96, 97, 99, 152, 154, 155, 162, 166, 167, 190, 191, 192, 232, 233
Kigoma, 127
Kikuyu, 16
Kilimanjaro, 30, 31, 34, 48, 63, 84, 176, 230, 232
Kilimatinde, 72
Killindini, 50, 52, 133, 137, 140, 211, 215
Kilossa, 90, 91
Kilwa, 89, 93, 97, 103, 105, 106, 107, 108, 109, 110, 111, 136, 139, 195, 232
"King of Maktau," 211
King's African Rifles, 23, 24, 26, 28, 40, 43, 60, 61, 65, 77, 96, 99, 106, 110, 113, 123, 126, 130, 134, 137, 158, 197, 198, 199, 200, 201, 202

Kisumu, 17
Kitchener, Lord, 49
Kondoa Irangi, 66, 68, 69, 70, 72, 73, 74, 102, 149, 169, 172, 176, 195, 219

LATEMA, 64
Lettow, Von, General, 67, 68, 70, 71, 72, 79, 80, 86, 104, 107, 108, 109, 110, 111, 112, 113, 114, 115, 116, 126, 127, 128, 129, 139, 141, 149, 158, 216, 217, 222, 223, 224
Lindi, 89, 93, 103, 105, 107, 108, 109, 110, 111, 117, 126, 135, 136, 139, 141, 182, 215, 229, 232
Liwale, 89, 111
Lol Kisale, 66
Longido, 31, 34, 62, 63
"Loppy," 212
Lorenzo Marques, 52
Lucinje, 125

MAGADI, 96
Mahenge, 89, 107, 110, 126
Malleson, General, 64
Masai, 26, 66, 176, 177
Massassi, 108
Mbuyuni, 61, 62
Medo, 118, 120, 160
Mikandani, 117
Mikesse, 89, 91, 157
Mingoyo, 103
Mohoro, 93
Mombasa, 17, 19, 34, 53, 151, 157
Morison, Sir Theodore, 179
Morogoro, 72, 73, 76, 77, 84, 157, 230, 232
Moschi, 30, 34, 48, 63, 64, 65, 66
Mozambique, 121, 122, 125, 139, 140, 141, 142
Mpangwas, 89, 90, 91

INDEX

Mpapua, 96, 176
Muanza, 78, 95
Muthaiga Club, 152
Muthaiga hospital, 220

NAIROBI, 19, 22, 25, 34, 61, 62, 151, 152, 157, 158, 170, 172, 176, 180, 190, 210, 220
Naivasha, 22
Nakuru, 22
Namirrue, 123
Native Labour Corps, 134
Naumann, 96, 178
Ngomano, 111
Nigerian force, 77, 89, 95, 107, 108, 109, 113, 134, 160
Northey, General, 116, 141
Nyasaland force, 23, 60, 89, 95, 108, 121, 126, 141

PANGANI RIVER, 34, 66
Persia, s.s., 50
Port Amelia, 117, 118, 120, 121, 135, 138, 139, 141, 160, 162, 211
Portuguese East Africa, 98, 104, 110, 112-131, 149, 160, 192
Pretoria, 51, 52
Pretorious the Scout, 216, 217

QUELIMANE, 122, 123, 135

RHODESIA, 126, 135, 167, 222
Rhodesian force, 60, 126, 134
Rovuma River, 103, 104, 107, 110, 111, 112, 114, 115, 124, 125, 126, 141, 222
Royal Fusiliers, 25th (The Frontiersmen), 60, 151
Ruaha, 90, 91
Rufigi valley, 77, 78, 81, 83, 84, 86, 87, 88, 89, 91, 95, 96, 100, 104, 149, 177, 182, 195

SALAITA, 35, 61, 62, 64
Sami, 96
Saxon, s.s., 50
Schnee, Von, General, 110, 128, 129
Scott, 41
Seychelles, 135
Simpson Baikie, 40, 57
Smith-Dorrien, General Sir Horace, 38, 39, 40, 51, 56, 57, 59, 65, 144
Smuts, General, 37, 56, 57, 58, 59, 60, 61, 62, 63, 65, 72, 83, 84, 85, 87, 99, 100, 102, 130, 144, 169, 198
Somalis, 23, 197
Songea, 89, 95, 108, 114, 115, 126, 222
South Africa, Union of, 37
South African Force, 47, 59, 61, 62, 63, 65, 69, 72, 77, 83, 102, 130, 134, 152, 172, 219, 220

TABORA, 67, 74, 76, 77, 78, 80, 84, 95, 127, 227, 229
Tanga, 30, 31, 34, 36, 53, 73, 84, 96, 212, 215, 230, 232
Tanganyika, Lake, 126, 127, 222
Tanganyika Territory. *See* German East Africa
Taveta, 34, 35, 59, 61, 62, 63, 64, 84, 151
Tighe, General, 58, 59, 64
Trent, s.s., 52
Tuna, Captain of the, 215
Tunduru, 89, 108

UASIN GUISHU PLATEAU, 20, 26
Uganda, 16, 17, 18, 23, 24, 27, 29, 31, 34, 42, 60, 61, 84, 151, 152, 159, 207

Ujiji, 78
Usambara, 30, 34, 69, 71, 73, 84, 169, 176, 220, 232
Utete, 89, 93

VAN DEVENTER, GENERAL, 99, 102, 129
Verbi, 45
Victoria, Lake, 16, 17, 31, 61, 78, 217, 232
Voi, 34, 61, 151

WAHLE, GENERAL, 227
Wavell, 26
Wedgwood, Major Josiah, 46
Wilhelmstal, 230
Wintgens, Major, 95, 96, 114, 178

Y.M.C.A., 173

ZANZIBAR, 143, 200, 229
Zanzibar, Bishop of, 135